DISC
NEW EARSWICK

Essays from
The New Earswick Bulletin
2000 - 2007

Elisabeth Alley

First published in 2009 by William Sessions Ltd
The Ebor Press
York

ISBN 978-1-85072-393-6

CONTENTS

Preface

In writing articles for the *New Earswick Bulletin* my research led to some fascinating discoveries about New Earswick, both past and present. Seven years later it seemed a natural progression to make a selection of these essays (plus contributions by others), arrange them according to their different themes and publish the result in book form. Excerpts from the Parish Council records have been inserted to provide background information.

The purpose of the book is threefold: first to record what I happen to have discovered about the results of Joseph Rowntree's social experiment a century after he set it up; secondly to raise funds for the continuing publication of the *Bulletin*, which provides an important service to residents of the village and indeed the whole parish; and thirdly to provide source material for the schools of New Earswick in the hope that their pupils may develop a sense of belonging to this unique place.

I am especially grateful to the New Earswick Community Association for sponsoring the book's publication, and there are many other people I wish to thank for the help they have given so willingly. These include staff of the Joseph Rowntree Housing Trust and the Foundation; officers of the City of York Council; long-established residents of New Earswick; and even the Serjeant-at-Arms at the Palace of Westminster. For his constant encouragement throughout the time I was writing for the *Bulletin* and since then, for his help in the production of this book, I would like to thank Richard York. Of course, no list of acknowledgements would be complete without mentioning my husband Ray, who insists it will suffice for me to thank him for his forbearance!

Elisabeth Alley
New Earswick, 2009

How it all began

Model Villages (January 2002)

The main inspiration for the garden villages we see today came from Ebenezer Howard's book *The Garden Cities of Tomorrow*, published in 1898. The creators of New Earswick and Bournville based their plans on Howard's ideas, and indeed consulted together on how best to put these ideas into practice.

Both Joseph Rowntree and George Cadbury were especially fortunate in having the wealth to realise their dreams, the source of these riches being cocoa. George Cadbury wrote, 'I have seriously considered how far a man is justified in giving away the heritage of his children and have come to the conclusion that my children will be all the better for being deprived of this money.' Joseph Rowntree believed that 'money is best spent by persons during their lifetime.' He recorded his great satisfaction that the trusts he established had the cordial assent of his wife and children.

Contrary to what many people think, neither George Cadbury nor Joseph Rowntree created their villages solely for the workers in their factories – unlike Saltaire built by Titus Salt some years earlier, or William Lever's Port Sunlight. The object in building New Earswick was 'to alleviate the condition of the working classes by provision of improved dwellings and organisation of village communities.' George Cadbury's aims were similar: 'the amelioration of the condition of the working class and labouring population ... by the provision of improved dwellings, with gardens and open space, to be enjoyed therewith.'

George Cadbury launched his trust in 1900. At that time it consisted of 313 houses built on 330 acres (having begun with 120 acres, much the same area as New Earswick) and it was worth £172,000. Now its population is over 20,000. New Earswick remained a relatively small development.

The two villages differ in appearance as well as size. Bournville lies in rolling countryside which, with its mature trees, gives it a natural attraction. The older parts of New Earswick (Western Terrace and Ivy Place for example) are very pleasant, but there's no denying the flatness of the landscape. In planning their villages, both men wanted something better than the long terraces of back-to-back houses which were a feature of industrial towns. Instead, they planned to have cottages, or semi-detached houses, or terraces of not more than four dwellings. In keeping with the garden village theme, roads were named after trees.

In her book *The Chocolate Conscience*, Gillian Wagner writes that Joseph Rowntree 'sought to create a village community which was to have nothing charitable about it, where tenants would pay rents which would give a practical return.' As for the houses themselves, he stipulated that they should be 'artistic in appearance, sanitary and thoroughly well built, yet within the means of a working man earning twenty-five shillings a week.' By 1914, Seebohm Rowntree (Joseph's son) could say, 'There is a little village outside York, two and a half miles from the middle of the city, with no means of transit except walking or bicycling along a muddy road, yet the houses could be let over and over again.'

George Cadbury had similar ideas, and to ensure a variety of style he employed different building firms, limiting each to no more than four houses. J.B. Priestley, who visited Bournville in 1933, described what he saw as a long road 'on which tiny villas have been sprinkled, as if out of a pepper pot.' He thought the inclusion of courts and quadrangles would have been better. The houses themselves struck him as being very superior, each one set in a large garden with fruit trees, as they were in New Earswick. Indeed the first houses in Bournville were such good value that their owner-occupiers sold them off at a handsome profit. Later houses were not for sale, but were let at between 6s and 8s 6d a week. Later on, after World War II, the Bournville Village Trust encouraged self-build societies, a policy which resulted in 400 new homes.

From similar aims, the two trusts have followed different policies, yet they continue to consult and confer. Furthermore, local authorities and housing associations have, where practicable, copied their ideas. As a result, the work begun by George Cadbury and Joseph Rowntree has spread far beyond the borders of Bournville and New Earswick. They would be surprised – and no doubt delighted – to see Prince Charles following in their footsteps with his model village of Poundbury on the outskirts of Dorchester.

The First Trustees (December 2004)
It is only fitting that we remember the five men who helped Joseph Rowntree launch the enterprise we know as New Earswick Village. Following the death of his brother and business partner, Henry Isaac Rowntree, Joseph came to rely on his four sons – John Wilhelm, Seebohm, Joseph Stephenson (known as Stephen) and

Oscar – and on his nephew Arnold. These five young men contributed to the success of the family business, and in due course they all became Trustees of the Village Trust.

The Trust Deed was signed in December 1904 and John Wilhelm, the eldest son, was appointed chairman. After only two meetings of the Trust, he had to visit the United States to consult an oculist about his failing sight. On the voyage he developed double pneumonia and died in New York at the age of 36. Although he had always suffered from ill health and poor hearing, he had joined the firm when was was 17, and worked enthusiastically in

Joseph Rowntree with (left to right) Stephen Rowntree, Seebohm Rowntree, Arnold Rowntree, and Oscar Rowntree, 31 May 1923.

the gum, cocoa and chocolate departments. His biographer, Stephen Allott, quotes the results of a series of mixing experiments for chocolate coatings. 'Mr John' (as he was known to the men) graded them as 'Good', 'Better', 'Best', 'Not So Good' and 'Vile'!

There was another, deeply spiritual side to John Wilhelm. At the turn of the 19th century, he did much to revitalise the Society of Friends (Quakers), urging that 'modern thought must be accepted, both in science and biblical study.'

The next brother, Seebohm, lived to a ripe old age. The introduction to *One Man's Vision* (published in 1954) states: 'Apart from the Founder of the Trust, Mr Joseph Rowntree himself, the greatest single contribution to anything which had been achieved by the Trust had been made by Seebohm Rowntree. Not only was he one of the original Trustees in 1904, but over the whole period since that date his contribution to the housing and social problems of Great Britain and indeed of the wider world had been outstanding.' Public recognition came in 1931, when he was made a Companion of Honour. By then the success of New Earswick Village was clear for all to see.

Together with his father and elder brother, Seebohm initiated improvements in the terms and conditions of the employees at the Cocoa Works. In his opinion 'Tanner's Moat was hell' and the move to Haxby Road was a great opportunity to put their new theories into practice.

Like his father, who was deeply concerned about the effects of drink, Seebohm studied the *causes* of social evil, particularly poverty, amongst York families. This is why when someone asked John Wilhelm 'Which Rowntree are you?' he replied, 'The son of Drink and the brother of Poverty!'

The next brother, Stephen, studied at Cambridge and was particularly interested in education. He undertook the management of the primary school and later the secondary school in New Earswick, faithfully compiling detailed reports year after year. In appreciation of this service, the metal gates erected at the original main entrance to the secondary school (on the south side) were known as the Joseph Stephenson Rowntree gates.

Oscar Rowntree is perhaps best remembered for his civic service. At 26, he was elected to York City Corporation. Nine years later he became Sheriff, then an alderman in 1920, and Mayor at the time of the General Strike. This was the year in which he 'earned universal appreciation for the brilliance with which he performed his many civic functions.' (*Cocoa Works Magazine*) Two others of those first trustees also served their local communities. Stephen was Mayor of Harrogate and Cousin Arnold was elected MP for York in 1910.

Once described as 'a big man with a big heart', Arnold was full of energy and bright ideas, finding his natural niche in advertising and sales. Apart from company business, his many other activities took him away from York on long train journeys. He used this time to write letters and even to consult with colleagues. As MP for York he worked hard to improve the conditions for railway workers. In World War I he helped to establish the rights of conscientious objectors and was involved in the formation of the Friends' Ambulance Unit. The minute recording his retirement from the Board states that 'he inspired all to do their best.'

Each with his own particular talents, those first Trustees formed a remarkable team.

CHAPTER ONE

2002: The Village Centenary

At its meeting of 21st January 2002, New Earswick Parish Council minuted the following:

> 'The Joseph Rowntree Housing Trust held a very well organised 'brainstorming' meeting for residents to come up with suggestions of how best to celebrate/commemorate this year as the year when Joseph Rowntree first purchased land for the village to be built on. These suggestions are being analysed and further meetings will be held in the near future. A sum of £35,000 has been allocated by the JRHT.'

A Centenary Thanksgiving Service for Joseph Rowntree's vision in creating the village of New Earswick took place on Sunday 26th May. Representatives from churches, schools and other organisations were asked to make very brief contributions. The chairman of the Hartrigg Oaks Residents' Committee at that time, recorded the following statement in the *Hartrigg Oaks News*:

> 'I have been asked to give thanks on behalf of the residents of Hartrigg Oaks, the newest development in New Earswick – we are only four years old.
>
> When Joseph Rowntree set up his Trusts, he gave his successors very wide powers to enter fields of service which he could not foresee. One of those successors was Erica Vere, who served as a trustee for 22 years. During that time she became an

enthusiastic supporter of the concept of a continuing care retirement community.

Just before she died, she wrote to the future residents of Hartrigg Oaks, pointing out that much of its ethos, its vitality and its effectiveness was in our hands.   It is for us to live up to these expectations: to continue the vision.'

Each participant was asked to bring a small symbol with them and to place it on the front table.   For Hartrigg Oaks, a sprig of oak leaves was chosen and placed in the vase already on the table.   This had been given by Primary School pupils to the residents of Red Lodge.

Let's Talk – Let's Listen was the title of a meeting held for residents of the Joseph Rowntree Housing Trust and the Bournville Village Trust to celebrate the New Earswick village centenary.

Tom Mannion, Chief Executive of the Irwell Valley Housing Association (Salford) was the main speaker and he treated us to a sparkling presentation.   Not only did he talk and we listen, but he gave us plenty to think about as well.   He quoted a saying of Einstein's: 'The logical mind can spot a wrong answer, but it takes a creative mind to spot the wrong question.'   When applied to arrears of rents in a housing association, it works like this: instead of concentrating on why so many tenants don't pay up on time, Irwell Valley Housing Association asked the question, 'How can we make it worth their while to keep up the payments on a regular basis?'

One of the answers was to institute a Gold Service – a system of rewards for prompt payment.   (Here I must report that Lord Best, in summing up, wondered if the rent had to be increased slightly in the first place in order to fund the annual £50 cash back!)   Other benefits in the

Gold Service include discounts (15% off the cost of a Co-op funeral), repairs carried out more speedily, and garden make-overs.

This Gold Service has been so successful that 86% of tenants now qualify for it. As a result, there has been a reduction in vandalism and nuisance and Irwell Valley Housing Association is now thinking of a Platinum Service.

On the subject of asking questions, Tom Mannion warned that if you ask tenants what they want, they will tell you – and sometimes you then have to do what they say!

The theme of talking to tenants, listening to them and acting upon their answers was taken up by Geoff Bunce of the New Earswick Residents' Forum. His example was that of modernising kitchens. Years and years ago, your kitchen was modernised regardless of your preference. The next stage was to offer three colour schemes, but everyone had to accept the majority choice, so the results were hardly individual. Nowadays, you have the colour you prefer and you can even choose not to have your kitchen modernised at all! It's taken a good number of years, but the talking-listening process has worked.

Asking the right question in that case was simple. But what are the questions we should be asking of our young people? This came up at one of the afternoon workshops. We heard from the Bournville youth leader and his team about how they had asked, not what makes pupils play truant from school, but how can we persuade them to make the most of their schooldays?

One of the answers was to reward a good record of attendance and generally keeping out of trouble with membership of an angling club. This popular project is called 'Get Hooked on Fishing' and was launched two years ago, thanks to the involvement of no fewer than 12 agencies and organisations. It must have taken a lot of dedication to get it going and it was the Bournville Village Trust that co-ordinated it. Some of the original members have now been put in charge of beginners. Another reward, based on similar lines, is membership of a cyber café.

Our own New Earswick young people talked about the Sleeper Path Project and how they encourage others to play football in their spare time. The girls have formed a Young Women's Group to discuss the many challenges they face as they grow up. What came through from all those who spoke at this workshop, whether from Bournville or New Earswick, was their sense of fulfilment – and their sense of fun.

White and blue Centenary Mugs distributed to residents and staff.

My one complaint is that there wasn't enough time. Not enough time to study the excellent displays (21 of them), not enough time to ask questions, not enough time for the informal exchange of ideas and opinions. But it was a good day. Who knows what may come of it!

Joan and John Addison took part in the **Centenary Air Photo** and Joan wrote this account:

June 1st 2002 – the Queen's Golden Jubilee, the start of the World Cup and, at New Earswick, an aerial photograph to mark the centenary of the founding of the village by Joseph Rowntree. This was to be no run-of-the-mill view of the village from the air, for down below something would be happening on the Rec. Residents and staff would be spelling out

New Earswick 2002

In a rash moment of community spirit we had signed up for this event, but as Saturday approached, with yet more rain and wind, we began to regret our rashness. However, Friday was a beautiful day and gave us hope, and when we opened the curtains on Saturday morning, the sun was already shining. We arrived at the Rec. at the specified time of 11.30 – stewards much in evidence, letters marked out on the grass, but it seemed an immense green space with very few people on it. The event seemed a non-starter. However, the stewards radiated confidence. A hundred and fifty had signed up, they said, and that would be sufficient if they all came and they were sure they would.

To begin with, we were positioned on the letters at two arms' length distance from each other. Someone on our letter suggested that this should have taken place on a week day and then a whole class could have been commandeered from the school! There were quite a few children who were gathered together in a group to sit along the lines of the numbers. They were remarkably patient.

By 12.30, more people had drifted along and we could be placed at one arm's distance (still not like that Halifax Building Society ad we'd had in mind). Now we were all wearing white paper hats and, indeed some people were already trying to repair them, as they were rather flimsy.

After this rehearsal, we were allowed to move, but warned to return to the very same spot by 12.45. Generous free tea and coffee were provided by Kippers fish & chip shop, and ice cream and cold drinks by Geoff Howard of the Happy Shopper. We returned to our places and passers-by were persuaded (or perhaps dragged off the street) to join us. At one o'clock, 200 white hats were on heads, the helicopter could be heard and instructions were obeyed (one hopes), to keep still, look to the front and, on no account, to look up. The helicopter circled round and round for what seemed an interminable time. Until then the waiting had been quite sociable and had that street-party feel, but this wait was tedious. Was the pilot satisfied with what he saw? We shall know when we see the result. Such a good idea and good organisation deserved to succeed.

Colin Cameron reported as follows: On 3rd June, **the 1902 house in Western Terrace** opened its doors to visitors for two weeks. The house proved to be popular with young and old alike, with just under 500 visitors. New Earswick Primary School booked three group visits and Haxby Primary School one visit. The house had also been extensively covered by the media. It closed on 14th June and was returned to Property Services in order for the modernisation to be completed.

The kitchen in the 1902 House.

Most of the artefacts were provided by a dealer from Harrogate, without whose help we could not have achieved such a realistic 'makeover'.

The New Earswick Story Group also prepared a small booklet describing life at the turn of the 20th century. It describes in graphic detail Monday's washing day and Tuesday's ironing day; then followed two days set aside for regular cleaning, and baking was usually done on a Friday.

Centenary Murals (November 2002)

The Joseph Rowntree Housing Trust wanted to commemorate particular aspects of New Earswick architecture, i.e. those parts which lie within the conservation area. They commissioned a set of murals from Pete Douglas, a community artist, to be displayed along the gallery of the Folk Hall Coffee Lounge.

'What *is* a community artist?' was the first question I asked when I interviewed Pete. He told me that his role was to encourage people of all ages to engage in art-based projects. These might be to commemorate an event, as in this case, or to enhance a building or to promote certain issues. He likes to work in a variety of art forms: murals, films and sculpture. He has just

Pete Douglas, in one of the murals.

finished a sculptural piece for the opening of the Tang Hall Community Centre – the casting of the hands of residents to make a wall relief.

For his New Earswick commission, he used a style called *decoupage*, which is very unusual for a mural. As the name implies, it involves cutting out shapes and mounting them on a background in such a way as to give a 3-D effect. Pete chose this technique to make the images of residents stand out against a background of the different styles of architecture typical of New Earswick.

It sounds easy, but it needs the artist's eye to achieve the correct scale and perspective, by selecting different sizes of figures. In one panel, there in the foreground is the head and shoulders of Vic Atkins turning to smile at the viewer. Yet to the left and *appearing* to be further back, is a row of children from the Little Rowans nursery group. These, and other figures, make a lively local scene in front of the houses of Western Terrace. Incidentally, when these children visited the Folk Hall to look at themselves and to identify other people in the murals, they soon spotted a familiar figure. 'Look, that's Mr Gales!' they said, turning to point him out on the opposite panel, which features the Hawthorn Terrace shops.

This is part of the enjoyment of these murals: looking for people you know and spotting the different backgrounds. Poplar Grove is there, so are the cottages in Lime Tree Avenue, the Swedish flats and the crow-stepped gable in Cherry Tree Avenue.

As is only right and proper, Joseph Rowntree himself appears in one panel. And by an illusion of time-travel, he is accompanied by present-day residents, Ian Cottom and Pam Smith. The latter, however, takes us *back* in time again, because she is dressed in the costume she wore for stewarding the 1902 house in June. The opening of this old house to the public as one of the centenary events explains why Sheelagh Loftus, who also helped with the stewarding, is wearing similar garb. She is to be found on the panel featuring The Garth, together with Jacquie Dale and Bill Briggs.

Pete told me that he is indebted to Pam Smith for taking most of the photographs. They were printed on high grade paper, but even so they were inclined to stretch in the mounting process. Meeting this challenge was greatly enjoyed by Pete and his two assistants, Gerry Solice and Linda Tomlinson. They also appreciated the encouragement they received from JRHT staff and the friendly co-operation of the Folk Hall management (yes, they are there too). In more ways than one, therefore, these murals are truly community art.

This Centenary Mural features Poplar Grove.

CHAPTER TWO

The Original Village

Conservation Area No. 20 (March 2006)

A large part of New Earswick was designated a conservation area in 1991. How does the process of designation work? In the first place, the proposal is drawn up by the Local Planning Authority and then put out for public consultation in various ways. Note is taken of the results and amendments may be made, after which it becomes embodied in the Local Plan.

The Local Planning Authority (for New Earswick back in 1991 this was Ryedale District Council) determines which parts of its area it wishes to preserve or enhance because of their historic interest, their character or appearance. A conservation area takes into account the area as a whole – both the built and the natural environment – and it may, of course, include individual listed buildings. Furthermore, the designation 'conservation area' is not a rigid one, and its extent must be reviewed 'from time to time.'

The practical guide issued to householders living within a conservation area states very clearly that 'the purpose of conservation is not about preventing all change but about managing it.' Thus, although our area is referred to as 'the original village' it has been possible to allow modernisation and improvement such as that at the southern end of Chestnut Grove and at the Elm Tree Garage site.

A look at this sketch plan shows how the boundary runs
north from Link Road along Haxby Road as far as White

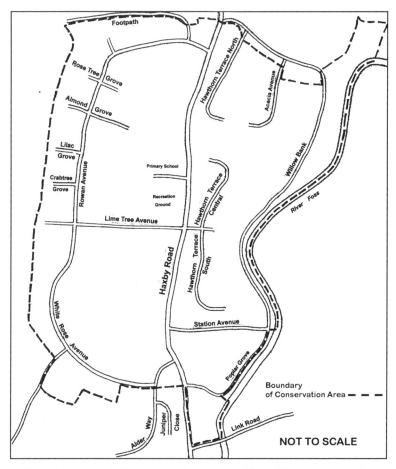

Sketch plan of Conservation Area No. 20, not to scale.

Rose Avenue.   This creates an interesting situation
concerning the avenue of sycamores which are a feature
of the southern approach.   Those on the east fall within
the Conservation Area but those on the west, in the rear
gardens of the Juniper Close properties, are subject to a
Tree Preservation Order.   To remove any of these

requires prior consent from the City of York Council (CoYC) who can ensure their replacement when necessary. CoYC is responsible for the trees in the highway verge and these were last inspected in January 2006.

The description of the buildings in 'the original village' departs from the business-like language used above and becomes almost lyrical: 'They are endowed with a character of their own and are essentially simple, yet are sympathetic to the rural setting; in spirit with the vernacular of the area, yet not a copy; rather an interpretation with an imaginative, consistent form and detailing to create a deeply satisfying sense of unity and identity.'

Places, Groves & Closes (February 2004)

The importance of the cul-de-sac is made clear in an article about New Earswick written in 1933 by the editor of *Town and Country Planning*, William Loftus Hare. He pointed out that the simplest way to develop the New Earswick site would have been to have about ten parallel roads running from east to west, cutting across the main Haxby Road. But Parker and Unwin, the architects, were anxious to avoid the regimented rows of identical housing seen elsewhere. They wanted something more individual, attractive – and economical. Their solution was the cul-de-sac, and William Loftus Hare described it as follows:

> 'The plan they prepared shows houses on the main and cross roads disposed in pairs, fours and sixes, well set back, with gardens back and front, and – for the first time – a large group of cul-de-sacs revealing advantages of importance. A short service road leads from the main road to a group of

say, twelve dwellings; footpaths connect each group. Thus, were brought into existence "Places" named after the sycamore, the rowan, the rose, the almond, the lilac, the crab and the cherry.'

The old method of site planning would have needed three cross roads for 36 houses, but the newer method reduced these roads by half. Furthermore, the 36 houses were arranged in attractive groups, rather than parallel rows. The result was a considerable reduction in the cost of the infrastructure and this saving was put into the houses.

It is interesting to note the cost of roads, sewers and services per house in Barry Parker's pre-war plan compared with his third post-war plan, the one with the cul-de-sacs. They were £56.13s.0d and £43.15s.11d respectively. Nor was the final plan just a saving in terms of money. Rowan Avenue would have had to be twice as long as it is now if the old-fashioned planning method had been followed. Where would it have gone, I wonder, for the fields immediately to the north were still part of Kettlestring Farm. (This purchase was not made until after the second World War.) The article in *Town and Country Planning* describes Rowan Avenue and its off-shoots as 'an excellent example of up-to-date and economical layout.'

We have to remember, of course, that in the years immediately after the first World War, few people anticipated the increase in car ownership. The narrow roads and shortcut footpaths are ideal for pedestrians and cyclists, but not for motorists, who require much more space for parking and turning, to say nothing of the need for surfaces capable of taking a greater weight. The increase in crime and anti-social behaviour is also contributing to a re-think about the desirability of the cul-de-sac.

When considering the names of these new roads, the word 'place' seems to have been dropped in favour of 'grove' and 'close', although Ivy and Rowan Places are a reminder of that early suggestion. 'Grove' proved a popular alternative; there are eight of them, including Poplar and Chestnut Groves.

For a change, 'Close' was chosen for 20 of New Earswick's cul-de-sacs, all of them in the newer parts. But we have come a long way from the days when it meant a small field or paddock enclosed by walls!

The following light-hearted piece was written in time for Christmas.

The Roofs of New Earswick (December 2006)

Landing six reindeer and a sleigh piled high with parcels on some of the roofs of New Earswick must pose quite a challenge to Father Christmas. Perhaps he finds time on his busy round to wonder why one small suburb of one small city should have such a variety of roofs.

Joseph Rowntree could have explained. In his plans for New Earswick, he wanted economy of building, yet with attractive and individual features. He liked the idea of terraces of four houses, each block being slightly different from those on either side. In other words, he wanted to avoid what the Americans nowadays call 'cookie cutter' housing; and his architects, Parker and Unwin, responded by producing some very ingenious designs, particularly for roofs.

Starting in the oldest part of the village, the roofs have steep gables (steep to an architect means more than 45 degrees) and their zigzag lines are interspersed with dormer windows. A striking feature in some of these houses, and notably in the Folk Hall, is the aptly-named catslide roof. This is where one part of the roof is longer

Catslide roof

than the rest. It continues at the same angle down to the top of a ground floor window or a door.

The shops on Hawthorn Terrace, with flats above them, were built in 1909. Their most striking feature is the two mansard gables, sloping steeply at the sides with a shallow pitch at the top. (The change of angle provides greater headroom on the upper floor.)

Attractive though these early buildings are, they were costing too much to be let at affordable rents: economies would have to be made. One suggestion was to simplify the rooflines and thus achieve a considerable saving in

Mansard gable over shops

the construction. At one stage, Joseph Rowntree even favoured flat roofs. However, according to Lewis Waddilove (writing in *One Man's Vision*) Unwin strongly objected, feeling this would be too great a loss in aesthetic appeal. Fortunately the other Village Trustees agreed with him, 'except for one or two experimental groups of flat-roofed houses mercifully hidden from general view in one corner of the estate.' In the course of time these proved to be unfit for their purpose and have since been replaced.

Thus it came about that the majority of houses in New Earswick have hipped roofs, though the architects cleverly introduced considerable variety. Hipped roofs are four-sided with a top ridge and as the name suggests, the cross-hipped roof has two parts that cross each other. There is an interesting variation on this theme at the junctions of Hawthorn Terrace and Rowan Avenue and Hawthorn Place, where the turn-end houses form an octagon. Developing the hipped roof style made this possible, without increasing the cost.

Hipped roofs are not so steeply pitched and they allow rain and snow to run off easily. An added advantage is that they make large eaves possible, thus keeping the drips well away from the walls. Many slope down to a slight curve, called an ear, whose purpose is to slow down the fall of rainwater into the drainpipe. Even here the architects turned this to advantage: the bungalows at the north end of Rowan Avenue have long elegant ears, forming graceful rooflines reminiscent of pagodas. The roof of Alder House is similarly designed.

One would expect the roofs with a shallower pitch to be better suited to Father Christmas's needs. In that case his favourite parking place might well be Sycamore Flats. But would the reindeer slither about on its copper panels? Another snag is the lack of chimneys for Father Christmas himself to use. Perhaps that's why he sometimes assumes an inflatable guise to climb the house wall and deliver his presents through the window.

But then I am forgetting that to a magical, mythical person like him, anything is possible!

The School Clock (April 2004)

At a meeting held in February 1911, it was resolved to accept the offer of an outside clock on the cupola of the primary school. It was donated by Joseph Stephenson Rowntree and his cousin Arnold, both of whom were

among the first Trustees of the Village Trust. William Potts of Leeds, tower and feature clockmakers, supplied the clock in 1912, the year in which the school was built.

Carole Farrar, the head teacher of the Primary School sent me a description of the clock (dated 1987) and copies of the company's worksheets for the previous 40 years. Although they have no record of the actual cost of the clock, they estimated it to be about £130 for the whole installation. At that time they had their own foundry, where the four dials were cast. These are just under a metre across, complete with raised numerals and minute marks, painted black against a white background, as we see them today. Striking every hour, the clock bell weighs about 38 kg and was cast at another foundry, John Taylor of Loughborough.

In 1946, when the cast iron dials needed to be replaced, white opal perspex was used and the circle of numerals and minutes (the chapter ring) was applied separately. The same procedure was followed for a second renewal in 1972.

The worksheets supplied by William Potts from 1947 to 1986 record the annual inspections plus repairs when required. Much of the detail is technical but some entries are easy for the layman to understand: 'bevel wheel taken away for new teeth, hands re-set' and 'bell re-positioned and nuts tightened.' More frequently it was a routine note 'oiled and examined', though on one occasion it was recorded that the oil was 'gungy'.

For nearly a century the clock has served New Earswick well, and is doing so again, in spite of fits and starts in recent years. It is the task of Walter Beavers, the Primary School caretaker, to wind New Earswick's one and only public clock. He does this once a week with a winding handle rather like the starting handles used for veteran cars, only rather smaller. Although the clock has four dials, they all operate from a shared central mechanism.

Of course, the weather vane has nothing to do with the clock, but it ought not to be omitted from this account. Made of copper, it represents a man reading a book to two children. Brian Jardine (JRHT Development Services Officer) informed me that it was re-furbished some time in the 1980s when the whole of the tower was restored, including the re-leading of the dome. There was discussion at the time as to who the man and the two children in Edwardian costume were. Was it a Quaker reading the Bible to the two children, as the schoolchildren of the eighties supposed? Would Joseph Rowntree and his sons and nephew have countenanced such an idea? After all, in his Memorandum of Foundation, Joseph took great care to emphasise the non-sectarian nature of the Trust.

One thing is certain: since its recent overhaul the clock is now in working order and, together with the weather vane, forms an attractive and useful feature in the centre of the village.

Going Green, describing how a conservation area can accommodate change (February 2004)

In developing the Elm Tree Garage site, the Joseph Rowntree Housing Trust sought a design which would contain 'a number of energy efficient measures and sustainability features.' In other words, the Trust is 'going green.' The challenge was to achieve this at affordable prices for the buyers and tenants.

Some of these energy efficient measures were incorporated in the earliest designs for New Earswick, particularly what is known as passive solar heating. In Western Terrace, advantage was taken of the west or south west aspect for the living room – a new idea, doing away with the separate and hardly-ever-used parlour. A through living room (from front to back) was designed for Poplar Grove and parts of Station Avenue to make the most of the available light for north and north-west facing houses. The same approach can be seen in both the primary school and the original secondary school building. Both have long south-facing elevations with ample windows.

The new development also takes advantage of passive solar heating by positioning the larger windows on the south and west, and the smaller ones on the other two sides. The build up of too much heat in the summer is avoided by shading, but the benefit of the winter sun can still be enjoyed. As for solar heating of the water supply, this will be done by panels on the southern slope of the roof, one to each house and flat. It won't supply all the hot water required, but it will certainly lower the gas bills.

There will be plenty of space on this southern roof slope to have photo-voltaic panels which generate electricity for other purposes. At present this is too expensive an option, but when the time comes it will be possible to fit the panels on to standard roof battens without much structural alteration.

Conservation of energy is important. Light fittings will be low energy; for heating, timers and sensors will play their part, and of course much depends on good insulation. This will be 30 cm thick in the roof spaces and 18 cm thick in the wall cavities. Wool, the best of all insulation materials, is unfortunately too expensive.

Water, too, needs to be used sparingly. Many New Earswick residents already have a rain butt and so will each Elm Tree Garage property. Use of rainwater for the garden and for washing the car is an old-established practice, but to be bang up to date it has been renamed 'rain harvesting'!

Inside, the WCs will be fitted with dual flush. The bathrooms will have flow restrictors on the showers and taps.

All the above will be evident to the occupants of the new development, but there are hidden factors to be considered. One of these is 'embodied energy', the energy which has gone into the building materials. Some use a lot of energy in their extraction or their manufacture, so cedar or oak cladding is planned for the upper walls. This echoes the timber gables on the houses at the southern end of Hawthorn Terrace. It fulfils another of the architects' aims: that of integration of the development into its surroundings. (Dormer windows and the low sloping southern roof will achieve a similar result.)

Recycling is also important in 'going green'. Not only will materials that have already been recycled be used where feasible, but also those which can be recycled at a later time, like timber and aluminium. The Trust is not averse to demolishing buildings to make way for something better, but would be reluctant to add to the problems of landfill; so plastics, foamed insulations and concrete are to be avoided.

In their design statement, Cole, Thompson Anders (the architects) say they were asked to design homes not only for the present, but for the future. This means allowing for changing environmental conditions. They have already proved in other parts of the country that high quality 'intelligent and green' homes can be 'affordable, attractive and can enhance neighbourhoods.'

New Earswick residents will have noticed that two prominent properties within the village, Westfield House and Hall Cottage, have been vacant for some time. Since both properties are listed buildings and in the heart of the conservation area, it has been important to involve the Conservation Officers from the City of York Council in any proposals.

The Trust has also been keen to demonstrate how the energy efficiency of existing properties can be improved. Both properties fail to meet the latest energy efficiency standards and a list of measures has been produced such as upgrading the thermal insulation and energy efficient boilers which will be included as part of the works.

Alterations to Westfield House & Hall Cottage
– by Jonathan Gibson (May 2007)

Westfield House. This former residential care home closed down some time ago. The current proposal is to convert it into four self-contained two-bedroom flats. This will involve a significant amount of internal alterations but little change to the exterior. The only noticeable change will be the creation of a private back garden and the link with Red Lodge will be severed.

Hall Cottage. To make best use of the available space Hall Cottage is to be converted into two semi-detached family houses, one for rent and one for shared ownership. Work will include an extension on the side of the property and each house will have its own garden.

Subject to planning approval, work is due to commence on both properties early in the summer and to be completed by Christmas.

CHAPTER THREE

The Natural Environment

Joseph Rowntree stipulated that 10% of his garden village should be open space – land apart from roads and gardens. The following article about the **Old School Playing Field** was written for *Hartrigg Oaks News* in February 2000, with help from Peter Walls.

Plans are afoot – and not for the first time – for the Old School Playing Field. As its name implies, the field was originally purchased by the Joseph Rowntree Foundation as a sports ground and was used as such from 1925 onwards. When the secondary school opened in 1942, its pupils had the use of the field; so did others, for example the junior teams from York City Football Club. The school now has sports facilities on its own side of the lane and most of the other users have moved elsewhere.

Today the field is appreciated for its own sake.… Up to quite recently there was a wild life area on the eastern side of the field with fairly mature hawthorn and dog rose, which together with young oaks and sycamores, made an ideal habitat for birds and insects. All this was readily accessible to pupils of both schools.

As the years went by, the demand for housing increased and Joseph Rowntree's plan for a garden village of about 100 houses had to be re-thought. Ryedale District Council, within whose boundaries New Earswick then lay, had already earmarked the two fields opposite the Old School Playing Field (popularly known as the pea and bean fields) for no fewer than 300 housing units! The Housing Trust also had plans – for 95 bungalows and a two-storey block of flats – on the Old School

Playing Field. These were to provide accommodation for a Continuing Care Retirement Community with a health care and administration centre. Landscaped gardens, a bowling green and a walkway giving access to the River Foss would be in keeping with the garden village.

But objections were lodged by New Earswick residents, who wanted to keep their 'mini green belt.' The objectors (649 from the village, 105 from the wider parish of New Earswick and 39 from other areas) wanted the Old School Playing Field to be properly defined as Green Belt land in order to give it the greatest possible protection against the development of any part of the site. The Parish Council asked for it to be designated common land.

The objection was upheld; in the Inspector's words, 'It retains, however, a visual importance because of its position immediately adjacent to New Earswick. Views across it and of it are so significant in this context as to merit protection.' This ruling did not apply to the two fields on the west of Haxby Road and they remained within Ryedale District's strategic plan for housing development, scheduled for after 1996.

Although the Trust would have preferred the Old School Playing Field for their Continuing Care development, they decided to build on the fields opposite instead. So their dream of 'high quality accommodation and attractive landscaping, with the provision of excellent care services' came true after all.

In the meantime there has been a change in local government boundaries. New Earswick has been absorbed into the City of York and is no longer part of Ryedale. The City of York plan gives environmental protection to the Old School Playing Field as green space

– but for how long? At the same time, there is a waiting list of 2,000 applicants wanting to live in New Earswick: where can they be housed?

It is hardly surprising that the attention of the Joseph Rowntree Housing Trust is focussed on the Old School Playing Field again. To build, or not to build? – that is the question.

The following issue of the *Hartrigg Oaks News* contained the results of the opinion poll run by the Parish Council; for planning purposes they needed to know the opinion of the whole parish, not just of the village.   The questionnaire went to everyone on New Earswick's electoral register and brought in a response from 1,152 people – 54%.   Of these, 891 opposed residential development, 134 supported it, 124 had no opinion either way, and 3 people did not state their preference. The report from the City of York Council (which conducted the poll) stated 'From a sample of this size the results accurately reflect the views of the New Earswick Parish, to within plus or minus 2%, with 95% confidence.'

Our Oldest Trees   (December 2000)

Having spotted the words 'ancient oak' on the architects' plans for the Old School Playing Field, I naturally wondered how old it is – and that means how fat it is. For, like many human beings, when a tree ceases to grow in height, it continues to expand, and this provides a rough and ready way of estimating its age. Of course to be really accurate one would have to wait until it is chopped down and then count its annual rings, but the following is a useful and very simple alternative.

According to the *Field Guide to Trees and Shrubs in Britain* (a Reader's Digest publication), a tree with a full crown expands, on average, by about 2.5 cm, or one inch, every year – if it is growing in uncrowded conditions. You simply run a measure round the tree at a height of 1.5 metres (five feet), and in no time at all you reach an answer. Using imperial measure, because it's easier, we found the girth of the ancient oak to be 13 ft. 8 in., which gave an age of 166 years. So it was back in the reign of William IV (Queen Victoria's uncle), that someone planted an acorn in the northwest corner of the Old School Playing Field. Or perhaps a forgetful squirrel had a store of acorns on that very spot, couldn't remember where they were, and one of them germinated.

Another old oak is to be found in the same field, growing near the mini-roundabout. It was difficult to measure, growing so near the fence and next to a hawthorn bush, but we found it dates back to the 1850's.

Younger still are the beech trees planted in what was once an avenue leading to the hall by Huntington church. These vary in girth. Two of the thickest measure 125 in. and 131 in., but in an avenue, one has to allow an increase of one inch every 18 months. Averaging the girth of these at 128 in., and then multiplying by 1.5, the answer came to 192 years. One beech is noticeably thinner than the others, and its age worked out at about 110 years, so perhaps that one was a replacement.

One final note about this method: if you want to use it to find the age of trees growing in a wood, say in the New Earswick Nature Reserve, you are supposed to allow *two* years for every inch of girth.

Felling the oak tree – by Audrey Steel (November 2006)

It is with great sadness that I have to report the passing of one of New Earswick's oldest residents – or rather, I should say the chopping down of one of our oldest trees, that is, the old oak opposite the entrance to Hartrigg Oaks.   Apparently the tree was not very well and was becoming a danger to life and limb.

However, one of the group of wood-choppers saw the funny side, and remarked that the elderly gentleman

taking photographs was probably the person who had planted the acorn in the first place.

It seems a pity to me that when an old tree is chopped down, there is no record or plaque to tell future children what this great tree had witnessed.   New Earswick children long gone must have climbed it and played with the acorns. Just think, this tree stood through two world wars and never wavered. Let's hope the wood is not just shredded and made into wood-chip!

Was it Queen Victoria or George II who was on the throne when our friend was planted? Should we inform the Palace? I hardly think so, but in my small way I salute a great warrior, who is now just a stump on the edge of a field.

More about oak trees (June 2007)

Sad though many of us were to see the mighty oak in the Old School Playing Field cut down last October, it had to be. Looking at the stump, you can see how the heart wood has rotted away. A telltale sign indicating the rotten

centre was the degree to which bracket fungus had taken hold.

The condition of the tree was assessed more accurately in April 2006 by sonic tomography, a technique first devised to assess the condition of telegraph poles. Based on the principle that sound waves move more slowly through decaying wood than solid wood, an image of the cross-section of the trunk can be generated. Sadly, it showed that only a small proportion of the wood remained intact.

Bill Briggs (Parks and Gardens Manager) tells me that the tree was so near the footway it presented a serious risk to the many pedestrians who walk along it. In keeping with good environmental policy, a couple of oak saplings were planted as replacements, but further away from the fence. They have since mysteriously 'disappeared.'

When the heartwood of a tree has rotten away, it is impossible to count all the annual rings and so determine the exact age of the tree. There is, however, the approximate method of measuring the girth at a height of 1.5 metres and dividing that figure by 2.54. Looking at old maps can sometimes confirm this estimate; for instance the three which still stand in the northern boundary hedge of the sports field are not shown on the large scale Ordnance Survey map of 1891. Mr Peter Hawley's estimate of 120 years is probably as near as we can get to the age of all three. (There was a fourth one originally.)

There are still a good number of younger, but mature, oak trees to be seen; one in the grounds of the primary school and five outside the secondary school, bordering Haxby Road. The latter must have been part of the Park Estate before it was purchased by the Trust. Oak trees provide food and shelter to over 200 creatures, ranging from birds, grey squirrels and wood mice, to many kinds of insects, particularly their caterpillars. Some of the latter gorge themselves on the young leaves, leaving them in such a state that a second leaf crop is produced in August. Others, like beetle grubs, live in the deep furrows of the bark, where green woodpeckers feed on them.

In olden times, acorns were of great importance as a food for fattening pigs. Their owners would turn them out into the forests every autumn to make the most of this free food. The right to do this was called pannage and it is still practised in the New Forest.

Acorns are well-known to be a favourite with jays and squirrels; they take them away to build up a store to see them through the winter. Not all the acorns are eaten and this accounts for oak seedlings emerging at some distance from the parent tree. Acorns that fall to the ground near the tree stand a good chance of germinating, because the leaf litter below the tree makes excellent compost. If you want to plant acorns, it is best to collect them in the first two or three months in order to meet with any success.

An oak tree is usually between 40 and 50 years old before it produces acorns from the male and female flowers which grow on the same tree. They can be seen in May; the male flowers are more noticeable, being pale green catkins. They swing in the wind, thus allowing the pollen to blow on to the much smaller female flowers which look like little buds, just behind the leaves at the tops of the shoots.

As the old saying goes, 'tall oaks from little acorns grow.' It is amazing that something as small as an acorn can grow into a tree 35 metres tall and which may live for hundreds of years.

Summer Spectacular (August 2006)

Every garden village features an abundance of flowering trees – but mostly in the spring. By July, the delicate white and pink of spring blossom has died off, and the brightness of the fresh young foliage has dimmed. So the sight of the Indian bean tree in full bloom comes as a real treat – a spectacular display of thickly clustered flowers, each one like a slightly frilly foxglove, creamy-yellow with purplish brown markings inside.

The New Earswick specimen is one of the many trees planted by Vic Atkins. In fact, it was the first tree he planted when he started work in the village as a lad of fifteen, and it is situated in what is now White Rose Avenue. At that time (1954), the area had been part of White Rose Farm and the site was being cleared to make way for housing. One of the gate posts of the farm entrance remains to this day in the hedge at Elm Tree Cottage and you can still see a fragment of paving where the drive led to the former farmhouse, now the Garth. As a result, the soil here is a bit gravelly, just right for the Indian bean tree, or *Catalpa bignonioides*. The sheltered site also suits this tree, for its huge heart-shaped leaves (25 cm by 15 cm) would otherwise become tattered in the wind.

The young tree was originally part of a big shrubbery, which included some conifers. Some 20 years later, when it began to flower, the rest of the shrubbery was cleared out and grassed over. Vic planted crocuses, supplied by Mrs Priestly of White Rose Avenue, around the base of the tree. These provide some welcome colour, contrasting with the bare branches and the bunches of long black seed pods. They are one reason for the name, Indian bean tree. First brought to this country from eastern central USA, 'Indian' refers to North American native Indians. The name *Catalpa* is thought to have been a mispronunciation of the name of the tribe (Catawba) in whose lands the tree was first recorded by British botanists early in the 18th century. The second part of its name, *bignonioides*, is taken from the trumpet vine *Bignonia*, which has similar leaves.

Because the heart-shaped leaves are so big, the weight of foliage on the spreading lateral branches is considerable and pulls them down. Vic tells me that when he first noticed they were splitting, he designed the necessary adjustable supports. Three of these were ordered from Richard Bell of Haxby (who has made the new gates for the Primary School). With continuing care like this, our Indian bean tree is doing well for its age – in spite of the fact that the gardening experts say it is best suited to conditions in the south of England!

Two Indian bean trees are more famous for their location than their condition: just outside the House of Commons in New Palace Yard. It was through our MP, Miss Anne McIntosh, that I discovered that it is the Serjeant-at-Arms who has the responsibility of looking after them. He told me he fears they are becoming very brittle and work is required to try and preserve them. He is now considering the viability of keeping the trees, having recently had to replace a couple elsewhere. In thanking him for this information, I sent photographs of our tree in full blossom, and he replied: 'It looks as if your tree is doing very much better than those in New Palace Yard.' However, the comparison is hardly fair – their trees were planted on top of an underground car park!

Foxes – a fact of life   (April 2001)

One snowy night last January, a Park Avenue resident noticed his security light suddenly switch on. Upon investigation, he saw a fox, just a few feet away, staring at him through the window. Then it turned and trotted away. Next morning he noticed its footprints in the snow, very like those of a dog, but with the middle toes much closer together. The tracks showed that the fox had come into his garden from the corner by Hartrigg Oaks, then into the neighbouring garden and out at the back to the fields of Kettlestring Farm. It has continued to turn up, usually in the early morning, and always seems to follow the same route.

Back in January, the fox, or it might have been a vixen, was probably on the lookout for a mate, for the mating season starts around Christmas and continues for several weeks. The cubs, just one litter per year, are born in March or April. Once independent of their parents, they roam around in their search for food, one of their routes being alongside the railway line, from where they can be heard barking to each other.

At this time of year they can be what Mr Lazenby of Kettlestring calls 'a bit of a problem' to the farmer. Lambing began in early March but well before that, Mr Lazenby brought all his sheep into the compound. Most years – when there is no threat of foot and mouth disease – he expects to lose only one or two lambs each year to foxes, and the number is kept as low as this because of his vigilance. But as soon as the ewes and their lambs are turned out again, the fields have to be patrolled. The foxes come late at night, looking for any weak lamb, or one whose mother lets it stray from her side. Then they bite its head off. Once Mr Lazenby found three or four foxes all at the same time waiting for a chance to kill. It's not just a question of looking out for foxes and scaring them off. If a sheep has died or if there is a stillbirth, the fox is quick to take advantage, so dead bodies have to be cleared away as soon as possible.

While foxes eat any small mammals, their diet is much more varied: birds of course, and during the summer months they eat beetles. In the autumn they make the most of fallen fruit. And all the year round they look for scraps we humans discard – yes, even chips left in bus shelters.

So there are probably more foxes roaming through New Earswick than we realise. Foxes are good climbers and if they climb over a garden gate or scramble under a barbed wire fence, we may find tufts of hairs left behind, particularly from May onwards when their winter coats begin to moult. For most people, the sight of a fox is an unexpected treat. I remember the first one I saw was in the middle of a town, calmly crossing the road in the evening rush hour! But to the farmer, the sight of a fox means action stations, 'for they are a fact of life and have to be dealt with…'

A walk on the wild side   (September 2003)

'Garden village' describes most of New Earswick very well, despite the attentions of the litter louts. The neatly cut grassed areas and the carefully tended trees and hedges are much appreciated, but I also enjoy the occasional areas left to Mother Nature. Early one July morning (because of the exceptional heat) I took a gentle stroll along Willow Bank: what, in my schooldays, we used to call a nature walk.

It was just the right time of year to see the blue sow thistle in bloom, about 70 metres upstream of the bridge. The flower is like a pale mauve daisy, about an inch across, and the leaves are edged with tiny prickles. It is

not at all common in the Vale of York or on the banks of the Foss. As it is so unusual, the City of York Yorkshire Museum's expert was called upon to identify it when it first appeared in New Earswick in 1996.

Some plants were tall enough to hold their own against the surrounding nettles, docks and tall grasses. Since the seeds have a silky 'parachute' they are wafted away on any passing breeze and may end up elsewhere in our area. The outlook is favourable for future generations, because the bees were busy pollinating the flowers, as were hoverflies and beetles.

Also giving great pleasure to visiting bees, were patches of great willow herb – not to be confused with rosebay willow herb or fireweed – growing by the river's edge. Another flower favoured by bees because of its pinky-mauve colour is the common mallow. There are clumps of this growing at the back of the garages.

Growing in the river was the yellow water lily, its golden globules rising a few centimetres above the water. The flowers are small, but its huge leaves are said to be the largest leaves of any British water plant. On the other side of the river is a scene like something out of *The Wind in the Willows*, where the gardens lead down to the water's edge.

There, perched on a piece of semi-submerged wood, was a moorhen, the red of its forehead and the base of its bill just visible in the deep shadows of the overhanging trees. Have you ever wondered why it's called a moorhen, when it is actually a water bird? The name isn't derived from the word 'moor' at all, but comes from the Anglo-Saxon *mor*, meaning a wet place or a mere; that makes much more sense.

The area between the river and the road soon widens out and becomes 'tame' again, with seats placed along its winding path. Some of the white (or Huntingdon) willows had been cut back and, judging by the state of the sawn-off branches, this treatment was sorely needed. The branches have since been cleared away, leaving the trees to recover from whatever was the trouble. Judging by the girth of their trunks, they could have been planted nearly a century ago and one wonders how much longer they will last. One of the advantages of this type of willow is that its roots bind the soil of river banks, thus helping to reduce erosion. Clearly, the care and attention they receive is a great benefit – even on the 'wild side'.

A humble little river   (January 2005)

After attending a talk entitled *My Vision for the Foss* given by the City of York Council's Countryside Officer, Bob Missin, I have been re-reading the excellent book by Michael Fife and Peter Walls about this 'humble little river', as the latter calls it.

The first part of the book, written by Michael Fife, gives the history of the river from Roman times to the present and concludes with a section on its future. Michael Fife sees its potential value for fishing, canoeing and riverside walks. He puts forward ideas for a full riverside walk of eight miles from York to beyond Strensall, where he would like to see the lock restored or converted to a canal museum, together with a 'tastefully built inn' which would be 'a worthwhile commercial venture and an added amenity.' (The final section of the book consists of suggestions for York City Football Club walks, contributed by David Nunns of the Ramblers Association.)

The middle section is by Peter Walls. As a naturalist, he provides a comprehensive survey of the plants and animals to be found in, on and beside the river. They range from willow trees to pondweed, from foxes to wood mice, from swans to wrens and from pike to sticklebacks; nor does he overlook insects, slugs and snails. Very helpfully, he lists them according to where and how frequently they occurred along the 20+miles of the river, before the 1972 widening scheme. Our stretch of the Foss, along the section shared with Huntington and flowing out again beyond Lock Cottage, is classed as the lower middle region. This arrangement makes it easy to check from Peter's list what we might still find locally along its banks.

River engineers, whose aim is to move water from A to B as quickly as possible, regard river banks as one way to achieve this. But Bob Missin reminded us that nature's way is to allow wetlands to act as a huge sponge, holding the floodwaters and releasing them slowly. Rivers are natural drains for the countryside and the Foss drains over 12,000 hectares of land to the north of York, according to Michael Fife. He points out that the volume of water is usually greater in winter, but sudden summer thunderstorms can give rise to dramatic fluctuations in the water level.

Back in the days when the river had potential as an important trade route, the Foss Navigation Company was founded. Canals were created to bypass the meanders and six locks were built to control the water level. Fifty years later, competition from the railways put an end to any hopes of commercial success for the Foss and years of neglect followed. Although York Council had bought the Company (for £4,000!) it was not until the end of the 19th century that work was started to clear the accumulated discharge from pig sties, stables and ash pits.

During the last century, various improvements were carried out to reduce polluting effluents. A modern sewerage scheme replaced the original one built in the early stages of New Earswick Village. Another major polluter, Hall's Leatherworks at Earswick Station, closed down and moved to Hull. All this and more is described in much greater detail in *The River Foss – its History and Natural History.*

Another scheme, of interest to us in New Earswick, was the widening of the river from 9 metres to 12 metres at Mill Hill, just south of All Saints Church. As can be seen in Peter Walls' diagram, the towpath was replaced by a flood plain and the adjoining land was levelled. Peter explains that several varieties of grass were sown; two of

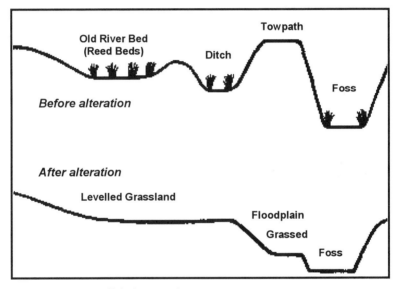

(After Peter Walls' diagram)

them were chosen for their ability to hold the soil when the river is in spate. Together with white and red clover, the plan was both to prevent erosion and also to provide suitable pasture for stock.

There are criticisms of the resulting park-like appearance, and Bob Missin described the Foss as a canalised river which has lost most of its wildlife interest. His vision, as our Countryside Officer, would be to increase the flood plain area and to restore the natural meanders. Well, he *was* talking about a vision, and 'where there is no vision, the people will perish.' In this case, it is the wildlife that would perish.

Tales from the River Bank (November 2007)

Starting at the north end of Willow Bank, Jeff Beavers (former New Earswick resident) and his wife Mary took me on a walk along the river bank.

The land, up to the first stile, is owned by the Joseph Rowntree Housing Trust. Indeed, in the very early days of New Earswick, Seebohm Rowntree had negotiated the purchase of that particular field so that an 'open tip' for village refuse and a sewage treatment works could be established. Jeff remembered a large diameter pipe used to carry the treated effluent to the river. As youngsters, he and his friends liked to run expertly along the top of this pipe, but one day he lost his footing and in he fell. His friends rushed away to tell his mother and by the time Jeff had scrambled out and run home to Sycamore Avenue his mother was waiting to give him a good sluicing down.

South of this pipe the land is now nicely landscaped from the back gardens of Chestnut Grove down to the river. But Jeff told me, 'Originally the land fell away sharply down from the back gardens to the river and here there were extensive reed beds. Growing to a metre or more in height they afforded great pleasure to us children in making dens and camps for numerous games and adventures.'

Pauline Crawford (*née* Freer) also has good reason to remember this part of the river bank. At the age of ten, it was the sight of yellow irises and cotton grass which tempted her to venture too far, and soon she was floundering in the boggy ground. Shoes and socks covered in mud, she tried to wash them clean – in the effluent pouring out of the pipe!

Beyond this area, Jeff, Mary and I climbed the stile, which they both remembered was once a farm gate, and then followed the meandering path. 'All along here' said Jeff, 'there were wild roses and we could leave our clothes under the bushes, when we wanted to swim. The water was about a foot deep at the edge and then you could wade out and dive into a depth of about three feet. This deeper water was called the splash. We all learnt to swim here. The fathers and older children taught the younger ones; we'd hold up their chins and they'd soon get the hang of it.' The course of the river has changed since those days, the wild roses have gone and the kingfishers are rarely seen.

Our next objective was to find where the stepping stones (or 'steppies') had been. On the way Mary told me that she and Jeff used to bring their children here for Sunday afternoon walks. She remembered one occasion, when their daughter Jill was about 18 months old and they'd all had a sleepless night as Jill was teething. They found a good place to sit, and it was so peaceful that all three fell fast asleep. But when they awoke it was to find themselves surrounded by a circle of very inquisitive cows! On the occasion of our walk, there were no cows, and no other people in spite of its being the first fine weather of the summer holidays.

On our left we passed a couple of very shallow ponds. Jeff and his friends used to have a great time fishing here for sticklebacks – three-spined, ten-spined and red-breasted. I'd never heard of the latter, but have since discovered that the male three-spined sticklebacks develop a red throat and belly in the spring.

Jeff also remembered there being a bridge here, brick-built with arches. As we wandered around we came across some brick paving nearby, perhaps traces of a farm track from West Huntington Hall.

We studied the opposite bank of the river and eventually Jeff made out the route of a steep cart track leading down from the road to the river, where the farmers used to bring their horses to drink. Looking up to the houses on the other side of the river we could see traffic on the road going uphill to some tall buildings, part of Manor Farm. We knew then that we were close to the site of the stepping stones. They have since been removed, but are shown in *New Earswick, A Pictorial History* by Joe Murphy. No doubt they were the setting for yet more tales from the river bank.

New Earswick Nature Reserve - by Brian Jardine, Chairman & Secretary to the Reserve (August 2000)

The wooded area to the south of the houses on Alder Way is the location of the New Earswick Nature Reserve, owned by the Housing Trust and managed by a committee of volunteers on behalf of the Trust.

The Reserve is the site of the brickworks that for many years at the beginning of the last century produced the bricks and roof tiles with which the houses in the Village were built. The works closed down in 1933, the kilns and other buildings dismantled and the area left to grow wild. The clay pit eventually filled with water and the pond, which is the central feature of the Reserve, was created.

In 1948 the Trust, following the encouragement of Wilfred Booth, the then Headteacher at the Primary School, established the area as a Nature Reserve for the local Schools to use for nature study. New trees and shrubs (all native British species) were planted and a fence was put around the area to protect them and the wildlife which quickly moved in.

In 1953 a Committee of Management was set up to oversee the Reserve and in 1955 official records of sightings started to be kept and this important work continues to this day. The records include lists of the species of grasses and wildflowers, birds, mammals, fish, insects, etc which have been seen in the Reserve and the meadow to the north east of the fenced area, which became part of the Reserve in 1993.

In the late 1960s an agreement was drawn up with the Local Authority giving the Reserve status as an Educational Reserve under the National Parks Act of 1949. A management policy was prepared as part of this, which still guides the work of the Management Committee today.

The pond has no natural stream inlet or outlet. It is replenished by rain and surface water run-off from the surrounding land and is therefore susceptible to fluctuations in rainfall. Records of water levels kept since 1982 show a difference of 642mm (24¼") between the highest and lowest levels. Either by natural or human means, fish were introduced into the pond, and it is now reasonably well stocked. New Earswick Angling Club has the fishing rights to the pond but a number of other anglers have been given permission to fish it by the Management Committee. Fishing is not permitted during the months of March to June inclusive, to protect the breeding wildlife.

The main purpose of the Reserve is to provide a resource for the local Schools and residents for the study of natural history and, of course, to provide a suitable environment for the wildlife living within it. For many years all the local schools made very extensive use of it for nature studies but this has diminished in recent years, for a number of reasons.

Because of the need to protect the wildlife from disturbance, and for reasons of safety (the pond is large and up to 12 feet deep), access to the Reserve has been restricted to the Schools, the Angling Club and those residents who have a particular interest in natural history. This situation will remain for as long as it is designated as an Educational Reserve.

The Management Committee is currently reviewing access to the Reserve and a more proactive management regime for it, to encourage greater use by the Schools and others. The Committee would welcome volunteer help to act as wardens, carry out minor maintenance tasks etc, to ensure that it remains a useful resource for the area and an interesting, enjoyable and safe place to visit while still providing an undisturbed place for wildlife to live and breed.

New Earswick Nature Reserve - by Brian Jardine, Chairman & Secretary to the Reserve (April 2004)

For about 25 years at the beginning of the last century, bricks and roof tiles for the houses then being built in New Earswick were made in the Trust's brickworks just to the south of the village. Production continued until the end of 1933, when the works were closed down and the buildings and machinery dismantled. All that now remains are the clay pit, the concrete base of an old wind-driven pump, a well and an area of brick pavement.

The pit gradually filled with water, creating the pond which can be seen today, and the area became 'wild'.

Parish Council Minutes:

> *July 1936:* Brick Pond smell – The clerk reported receipt of complaints about the offensive odour from the unused brickyard pond as a result of the dumping of gums by Messrs Rowntrees. A letter was sent to the responsible department at the Cocoa Works.

> *October 1936:* It was reported that the pond was now pumped dry and the offensive smell had ended.

Brian Jardine's account continues:

In 1973 a formal agreement with the local authority led to the area being established as a Designated Educational Nature Reserve 'whose object is to provide a place for the outdoor study of natural history.' Some years ago the Triangular Meadow was added to the Reserve; this small meadow to the west of the main Reserve along the old railway track is a good example of ridge and furrow meadow, which was once widespread in this country but is now diminishing rapidly.

The Reserve is managed by a committee, which includes staff of the Trust, representatives from local schools, the New Earswick Residents' Forum, the Parish Council and the New Earswick Angling Club, and a number of individual members. A Management Plan has been drawn up for a 5-year programme of maintenance and improvement, and the work is carried out by a number of volunteers who regularly give up their Saturday mornings to help. Additional helpers are always welcome.

Three Open Days are held during the year when visitors are welcome to look round the Reserve and Triangular Meadow. At the June Open Day displays about the Reserve are put on and the Angling Club gives demonstrations of fishing and sets up competitions for the young visitors. Roma Oxford often brings along

some of her 'Mobile Mini-Beasts' and last year organised pond dipping.

As a designated educational reserve, the Management Committee keeps very comprehensive records of the wildlife of the area, including birds (over 100 different species have been seen in it since record-keeping began more than thirty years ago), plants and trees, fish and pond life, mosses, galls, fungi and mammals. A bird-feeding programme continues during the winter and spring and nest boxes are provided. A new, small pond is being established as a habitat for amphibians such as newts and a new island has been created for nesting water birds. A network of stone paths is being laid to give access around the pond and through the woodland. New bird hides will be built over the next year or two, and a small resources building is planned where a permanent exhibition about the Reserve can be displayed.

National Nest Box Week   (February 2006)

National Nest Box Week starts on Valentine's Day each year, and right in the middle of that week the New Earswick Nature Reserve is holding its first Open Day of 2006. It is an excellent time of year to see a variety of nest boxes, while the trees are still bare. Although you may notice birds around the nest boxes, they are likely just to be house hunting and they won't actually start nesting in the box of their choice until a few weeks later.

Like ourselves, they are looking for something secure, weatherproof, and safe from predators. Nest boxes are made with holes of different diameters, the smallest being 2.5 cm. This keeps out the predators, limiting the occupants to wrens, blue tits, great tits, coal tits, and tree sparrows. Of these, the blue tits take most readily to nesting in boxes, and they're good little housekeepers too, clearing out the droppings of their young. Volunteers running the nest box scheme in the New Earswick Nature Reserve reported 100% occupancy in 2003, with blue tits nesting in 75% of the boxes and great tits occupying the remainder. In 2004 the numbers were down slightly for blue tits and up a few for the great tits.

The nest boxes are basically all the same design, with an overhanging roof to keep out the rain and an entrance hole high in the front. The inside walls have to have a roughened surface to give the fledglings a good grip as they scrabble up to the hole. Tilting the box slightly forward also helps the young ones, besides providing effective drainage. Larger birds need larger entrance holes: 3.2 cm to 5 cm diameter for woodpeckers. The woodpecker has a further requirement: some rotting wood from which it can dig out its nest, and it has been found that polystyrene is an acceptable substitute.

Nest boxes are usually positioned to face a northerly direction, so as to avoid direct sunlight and the heaviest rain. They also need to be placed well away from the feeding boxes (sited along the north-western path). This is because the constant to-ing and fro-ing of other birds discourages breeding.

The feeding boxes are much wider than nest boxes and are fronted with strong, square-mesh wire. Look closely,

and you will see the lower edges have been gnawed by that prettiest of pests, the grey squirrel. You will also notice a second piece of mesh has been fitted over the first so as to make the squares too small for the squirrel.

(Evidently the squirrels can squeeze through the standard size of mesh.)

Much larger than the nest and feeding boxes on the trees, are several duck boxes on the new island in the south eastern corner of the Nature Reserve facing the water. The gate on the new bridge leading to the island is kept locked so as to avoid disturbing the nesting ducks.

Walking round to the opposite side of the pond, past all the feeding boxes, you will come across two very unusual nest boxes, both of them painted black. The long rectangular one, angled at 45 degrees high up among the branches, is designed for a tawny owl. It is open at the upper end, ready for the tawny owl to swoop down into it. The aim is to mimic the deep cavity which would be its natural choice of home.

The other strange box is perched right at the top of a dead tree in the hope that it is just what a pair of barn owls might be looking for. The entrance hole in one of the bottom corners is about 15 cm square, and you can see a tray sticking out in front; this provides an exercise yard for the owlets. If and when a pair of barn owls chooses to move in, it may be as long as two years before any owlets come out to flex their wing muscles, for the adults may simply roost there before breeding.

As their name implies, barn owls choose old barns as breeding and roosting sites, but many of these have been knocked down, or modernised. Deep holes in tree branches, particularly elms, are also favoured by barn owls, but Dutch elm disease has reduced this option too.

Loss of habitat has led to a general decline in the bird population and it is good to know that voluntary schemes, like the one in New Earswick, are helping to reverse this trend.

House Sparrows in New Earswick (a contribution by Ian Nicholson, a member of the management committee of the Nature Reserve, June 2006)

There has been a considerable amount of publicity over the last couple of years about the plight of the House Sparrow. Not long ago, this was one of the commonest birds in Britain, and indeed, was regarded as a pest by many. Recently, however, the UK population has crashed dramatically, with the result that it is now quite a rare bird in some parts of the country. The decline has been most significant in the south-east of Britain, whereas in other areas there are still reasonable numbers of sparrows to be seen, although nowhere are they as abundant as they were 20 years or so ago.

Yorkshire is one of the areas least affected by this decline, and there is certainly still a fairly healthy population around New Earswick. The British Trust for Ornithology (BTO) is keen to investigate the reasons for the declining population, and as part of this investigation we intend to start placing coloured rings on the legs of the sparrows which we trap in the course of the ongoing bird-ringing programme in various parts of the village. In this way, by noting where and when the colour-ringed birds are seen, we hope to be able to monitor the birds' movements and habitat preferences at different times during the year.

The birds which are ringed will have a standard numbered BTO metal ring on the right leg, below which will be a coloured ring. The left leg will have two coloured rings. It would be very helpful if anyone who sees a colour- ringed House Sparrow around the village could make a note of the colours of the rings. It is important to note the position of the rings, for example yellow above red, or dark blue above light green, as this information is needed to identify the bird as an individual. Details of any sightings can be notified direct to the BTO website (www.bto.org) which has a section where ringed birds can be reported.

This project is an important part of the effort to protect one of Britain's most familiar garden birds, and any help which you can give by reporting sightings will be greatly appreciated.

House Sparrow (after F. Greenaway in *Reader's Digest Field Guide to the Birds of Britain, 1981.*)

CHAPTER FOUR

Services and Amenities

White Rose Dairy (September 2001)

Not only is New Earswick famous for being one of the earliest garden villages, it is also well-known as the scene of pioneering work in the production of clean milk.

It all began, not with Joseph Rowntree, but his son Seebohm who was particularly interested in public health. He was involved with the York Health and Housing Reform Association, which was set up in 1901. It was deeply concerned that the alarmingly high rate of infant mortality might be due to contaminated milk.

The source of contamination in untreated milk could be from the cows themselves or from handling the milk delivery. This reminiscence of the latter comes from Joe Murphy's book *New Earswick, a pictorial history*: 'Milk was delivered from our own cows at Crompton Farm by pony and float into New Earswick, two deliveries a day, 7 am and 4 pm, and woe betide any of us if it was late …Before I went to school I had to deliver many pints of milk, often out of an open can and with a ladle.' Hygiene couldn't be guaranteed.

As early as 1899, and on the other side of the Pennines, the Manchester Pure Milk Company had been formed. Its consulting expert was Wilfred Sorensen, who had arrived from Denmark where his uncle had a dairy business. He didn't actually own any farms himself, but purchased milk from carefully selected farms, and ensured its freshness by keeping it cool. Sorensen was invited to speak about his methods at a meeting of the York

Medical Society and that was where he met Seebohm Rowntree. The Manchester project was short-lived because the suppliers refused to meet the high standards of the Company. People preferred to have warm milk drawn from the cans of the town cowkeepers and delivered twice daily.

By now Joseph Rowntree's plans for the village of New Earswick were maturing. His purchase of land included a former stud farm, run by John Tebbutt. So it seemed a good idea to let this land and the farm buildings to Carl Sorensen, which allowed him to be a milk producer in his own right, controlling both the production of milk and its distribution. He started what became known as the White Rose Dairy with three cows, and soon increased his herd to 30 and then 50.

Of the help he received from Joseph Rowntree he said, 'He not only built for me a model cowhouse to my own design, but at considerable expense to himself had town water laid on to the farm a year or two before he required it for his own building schemes.'

Sorensen insisted on high standards of cleanliness. The milkers had to wear overalls and, before milking the cows, they had first to wash themselves and then the cows' udders. As another description in Joe Murphy's book says, 'everything was absolutely spot on, he wouldn't have any dirt kicking about, it was all cleaned and washed out every day when they finished with the cows.' The milk was filtered and then cooled sufficiently to kill any bacteria. Some of it was bottled on the farm; as for the rest, it was always drawn by tap from a sealed can. So Sorensen could truly boast of 'pure, clean, ice-cooled milk from healthy cows.'

Gradually, as the housing stock grew, less and less land was available. This had been understood right from the beginning, but unfortunately Sorensen was unable to find suitable land elsewhere. He rose to the challenge by making and feeding silage. After his retirement in 1940 at the age of 70, the dairy was run for a few years in association with another farm nearby. But housing had priority and 1946 saw the completion of the first part of the White Rose Estate building programme – the 12 old people's cottages in Lime Tree Avenue. By 1948, the year in which Sorensen died, his former home (The Garth) had been converted into a home for the elderly. The elderly of today, who were children in New Earswick when Carl Sorensen was running his dairy, remember how they used to call him 'Oslo' (with a fine disregard for geography!), and what a lot he and his wife did for the village.

The Yellow Peril, and other pre-war buses
(February 2007)

In the earliest days there was no bus service to New Earswick. People either cycled or walked to work – and

that was the Cocoa Works for most of them. Rowntrees calculated that this meant a 20-minute walk each way and accordingly they added an extra few pence to the wage packet. The first bus was run by Northern Motor Utilities and was known as the 'yellow peril'. It only went as far as the factory; if you wanted to go to the station, for example, then you had to change to a municipal bus, whose northerly terminus was also the factory. That was during the 1920s, after which came little red buses called 'Cosy Cars' and they were run by Sherriff and Mennell, who had a garage on the Wigginton Road. The Cosy Cars were single deckers and seated about 30 passengers. Small blue buses also provided a service for New Earswick residents and they were run by the People's Bus Service. As Joe Murphy has recorded in his *Pictorial History of New Earswick*, the considerable rivalry between the red and the blue buses did not bring about improvements in either service; both of them were chaotic. 'In those days there were no regulations specifying routes and stopping places ... They would stop to pick up or set down passengers anywhere, and if regular users were a bit late the drivers would stop at the

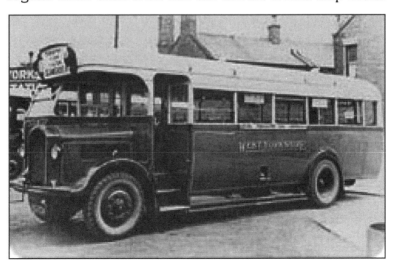

gate and blow the horn.'

These two small companies were bought out by the West Yorkshire Road Car Company. The routes were extended either to Piccadilly or to the station, and double deckers were introduced. This caused a great outcry because of the need to get through the bars; in the very first week one of them tried to drive through Monk Bar! Although regulations were now in place, there were still many complaints and in 1934 these were taken up by the newly established Parish Council. The Clerk was instructed to write to the bus company about the inadequate service on Saturday afternoons and evenings and also on weekday mornings. All were subject to serious overcrowding, for few people had cars.

In fact, the first New Earswick resident to have a car was Councillor Arthur Minney who lived in Park Avenue. Together with Councillors Hallaways and Wragge, he was appointed to 'watch closely the efficiency of the bus service.' A notice was inserted in the Folk Hall monthly sheet (forerunner of the *Bulletin*) asking for reports of specific complaints.

The following month, council representatives had an interview with the Traffic Manager of the bus company, but to little effect. The Parish Council minutes state: 'These unfortunates had left the interview dazed by a flood of oratory... The general opinion was that the position was even worse than before the interview.' Besides the frequently inadequate service, some buses were even departing before the scheduled time.

Nothing daunted, they approached a higher authority, the Traffic Commissioners. Flaxton Rural District Council was already protesting against increased rates for contract tickets (i.e. for 12 journeys, weekly and monthly). Haxby Parish Council was invited to campaign with New Earswick against increased fares and deficiencies in the service. Soon Strensall, Wigginton and Huntington joined in the formation of an inter-council traffic committee.

In order to present the outstanding complaints and difficulties more clearly, Mr Minney prepared a mileage cost chart. The bus company based its charges on 0.8d (old pence) return per mile, yet Mr Minney's chart showed that New Earswick passengers were paying 1.03d per mile over the full journey. Another injustice was the fact that Village residents could get a return ticket to York for 5d, but this was not on offer to those living in Park Avenue – they had to pay for two single journeys at 3d each.

At Mr Minney's suggestion, each council then held its own public protest meeting and it was reported that there was a definite improvement following the meetings. In October of that year (1936) the bus company offered some concessions: reduction of fares and some modification of the timetables. But as for the request to provide shelter for passengers at the principal bus stops, they disclaimed any responsibility for this.

Now, nearly 70 years later, as I wait in a council bus shelter, having checked First York's timetable for the arrival of the next bus (usually on time), I can appreciate how much the service has improved since 'the good old days'.

Adapting to Changing Needs: the Folk Hall (April 2007)

The need for 'a place for meeting', as Joseph Rowntree called it, was first met in 1904 when a couple of houses were set aside for use as the 'Assembly Rooms'. This accommodation soon proved too small for the various religious denominations to hold their services, and so the

Folk Hall was built – the original hall, as shown in John O'Connor's wood engraving.

Costing £2,278 15s. 1½d. to build, it was the gift of the Joseph Rowntree Village Trust; the Village Council would meet the running costs.

Originally, the main hall was where the coffee lounge now is and upstairs there was a meeting room, a library and a reading room; most villages had these amenities a hundred years ago. But within 30 years a bigger hall with a stage was needed, particularly for productions by the Operatic Society. So alterations and extensions followed, though they had to wait their turn as the main priority was housing. There were also changes in the use of the premises. The Methodists had their own chapel, and St Andrew's church was built for the Anglicans, both of them on land donated by the Trust; the Catholics and lastly the Quakers left later on. A separate library, opening in 1975, released room in the Folk Hall for other purposes.

Social activities were also changing as the century progressed, with the advent of radio, cinema, and then television. Increased car ownership made it easier for villagers to go out of New Earswick for their entertainment – to the Indoor Bowls Club, for example, at Tanner's Yard. And, as their advertisement says, 'It's not just for Bowlers!'

In his opening address, Joseph Rowntree hoped the Hall would become the Village Club with many interests and activities naturally centred there. One of his suggestions was for 'popular lectures with the Magic Lantern.' He also mentioned 'the tea gardens and public resorts in Germany, where the man and his wife and often their

children, would spend the evening together listening to the music. In this country,' he continued, 'it seems to be thought that women do not need recreation.'

What would he have thought of the popularity of dances which peaked in the 1940s? Saturday evenings used to be reserved for them and they were so successful that by 1948, the admission price was doubled in order to keep the numbers down! Nowadays there is dancing on Monday evenings and tea dances take place on Friday afternoons. Indeed, the maple dance floor in the 1935 hall was listed as a major asset in a survey conducted ten years ago by Community Matters (the National Federation of Community Organisations, a registered charity.)

Among the many other advantages mentioned were the central location of the Folk Hall and the large free car park. (It provides spaces for 95 cars and there are plans to reorganise it.) The importance of the car park had been recognised some years earlier by the Village Council when they ran a very effective promotion campaign to attract bookings from organisations outside New Earswick.

Residents mentioned these opportunities again in the 1996 survey, but also 'difficulties in reconciling the need for income generation against community usage.' The décor and furnishing were thought to be plain and old-fashioned and some people considered the hall too big for the community. Yet it comes into its own for Christmas parties, and wedding receptions; nor must we forget the recent visit of the Prime Minister whose speech was delivered to a packed audience in the hall.

Negative aspects shown up by the survey were the complaints that 'residents don't want to pay for anything', and 'it was difficult to get people involved.'

The range of rooms available for hire was seen as an advantage, but the layout is confusing, and there is little to guide the first-time visitor. Suppose you want to attend a meeting of the Parish Council: how do you find your way there? Enter the building from the car park; go past the reception desk and turn left into the passage alongside the coffee lounge; at the end, turn right up the stairs; the meeting room is on your right, but you must turn left along the balcony overlooking the coffee lounge; go through a doorway at the end; turn right past the office annexe, then left along a rather dark passage, finally through a narrow doorway – and there you are!

New Earswick Primary School (June 2001)

New Earswick Primary School was opened in 1912, a year in which the Suffragette campaign was in full swing. The occasion provided an ideal chance to publicise their cause, for the guests of honour included the Rt. Hon. Walter Runciman and Joseph Rowntree. That meant the press would also be there.

Every precaution had been taken against disruption and the car bringing the visitors had driven into the schoolyard. The gates were firmly shut and two plain clothes men were on duty, one of them from Scotland Yard. But at the end of the proceedings, the car had to be driven out again and one suffragette – Miss Violet Keys Jones – seized her chance and tried to jump on the running board. The security men grabbed her and the ensuing scuffle nearly landed all three of them in the mud. In spite of being outnumbered, Miss Keys Jones managed to break free and began to run after the car. Of course it was hopeless, so she very sensibly gave up and rejoined her companion. Then, according to the account in *The Yorkshire Herald*, the two of them were invited to tea by a sympathiser.

Skool Daze   (January 2005)

In November 2004, Geoff Bunce went back to school for a day, and wrote about his experience as follows.

I wanted to spend a day as part of my duty as a School Governor, and I was certainly impressed by the modern day methods of teaching. The school felt warm and friendly with the 'meet and greet' reception before lessons started. The desks, classrooms, corridors and hall have not changed significantly since I attended many years ago, but the teaching methods – what a refreshing change!

In Maths, the children were taught by using number fans and spider legs on the blackboard, while each child had a whiteboard and a marker pen which they used to solve mathematical problems, rub out and do the next one. In English, the pupils were given words for which they had to write a dictionary definition; but halfway through, at a signal from the teacher, the class stood up and copied actions to a well-known popular disco song, sat down again and continued with the theme of words. The children were all attentive and gave readily their versions of the word on the board.

For Story Time it was the 'Remembrance Day' theme, and these children gave accounts of events in the war as if they had been there. All took great pride in wanting to join in the discussion and writing. Science was not on the curriculum when I attended, but now it is introduced into the lessons without the children realising it is Science. This particular day, with the rain pouring down outside, the topic was sunshine and the shadow-lengths cast by the sun. Not much chance of participation then? Wrong! The class moved into the hall for some children to form a circle and others, representing the sun and moon, to move round the circle demonstrating the earth's movement.

The day finished with swimming lessons at New Earswick Pool, where each of the infant classes took turns in the water. Some were early learners, others more established swimmers, but they all gave their best and it was pleasing to see the parents on the balcony giving their encouragement and support to everyone.

A wonderful day and a treasured opportunity to see for myself the Primary School from within. Thank you, children and staff, for making me feel welcome; I enjoyed every minute.

My School Visit (August 2005)

The following year Geoff reported on another visit, this time during Healthy Schools Week:

The week involved not only healthy eating but also sensible exercising and explanations about the environment and the local community.

I witnessed many forms of exercising during the day – walking, running, dancing, tag rugby and gymnastics, as well as lessons on the effects of asthma in children and adults. A visit to the local supermarkets at Monks Cross had been arranged for some classes to see first hand the variety of fruit and vegetables available and learn from their staff about the goodness of organic food and the detriment of too many fizzy drinks. During the morning break all pupils received free fruit, the Government paying for the infant fruit and donations from the community to cover the junior pupils.

The children certainly enjoyed themselves and this proves conclusively to me that giving the option to exercise brings benefits in the classroom to concentrate on learning.

The whole week involved a lot of work in preparation and thanks go to the large number of people, staff and parents who volunteered to put the programme together and to those who took part in the activities during the week. Well done.

Dinner date – an account of the author's visit to the Primary School (May 2007)

Imagine my surprise when I was shown into the school hall which serves as the dining room: far from being a scene out of *Oliver Twist*, it presented a most attractive

picture. Little green chairs were set out round eleven circular tables, at which sat children of assorted sizes. Their tops, some red, some navy blue and others light blue, added more colour to the scene and the whole was illumined by what must be the largest and most beautiful window in the whole of New Earswick, its arched top reaching almost to the ceiling.

This, then, is the setting for the new policy of 'family service style dinners', which began last September. Instead of queuing cafeteria-style for the whole meal served on a plastic tray, the food is now brought, one course at a time, by the school dining room assistants to each table. Here it is served out by two older children; they later stack the empty plates and the dining room assistants then carry them away and put them in the industrial size dish washer. For the first course, we had fish fingers, mashed potatoes with cheese sauce, peas and sweet corn, all cooked on the school premises. This was followed by home-made sponge pudding and custard, with fresh fruit as an alternative. The menus are based on a three-week schedule brought out by North Yorkshire County Caterers. Remembering my own dislike of school cabbage, I noted that it appears only once each week. Main courses always include two vegetables, so there is a choice. As well as traditional offerings like toad in the hole and chicken casserole, some more exotic dishes appear on the menu – tuna pasta bake, turkey stir fry with rice, and cheese and tomato pizza, for example.

The children's appetites have improved and waste has been reduced. Under the former system, where the whole meal was served at the same time, some children might have been tempted to eat their pudding first.

(What effect would that have had on their digestive systems, I wonder?)

Out of the 210 children who attend New Earswick Primary School, about half stay for lunch. Not all of them stay every day; they book their lunches on Mondays for the coming week. Some of them bring a packed lunch and eat it in a separate room, and some go home.

At my table there were three year 6 pupils, one from year 3, and three from year 2 and, I should mention, Paul Hudson the chairman of the governors who kindly accompanied me. The selection of the two pupils in charge of each table and who should be seated at it, is done by the staff. It certainly worked well at our table – the older children conversed freely and easily with their visitors, besides keeping an eye on the younger ones. Mixing the age range is part of the family policy, and helps to maintain the new calmer atmosphere which now prevails. Even more important is the elimination of queuing and any temptation to push and shove. This is reflected in the reduced number of lunch time detentions. A detention, I was told, consists of being sent to the 'think about it' room to spend five or ten minutes pondering their misdemeanours.

As we left the hall, the dining room assistants were in action once more. This time they were wiping the tops of the swivel tables, tipping them up and wheeling them out to the furniture store situated alongside the hall. The little green chairs were stacked and removed. A huge mop made short work of the inevitable spills on the floor and very soon all was spick and span, ready for the next activity.

For me, the next activity was in the playground, where there is currently a serious shortage of space due to the building works. A temporary partition separated the infants from the juniors. Two mid-day supervisors look after the little ones, playing games with them. As I watched, the hokey-kokey was in full swing. The juniors also have two supervisors, and if anyone misbehaves they are given a red card – a lesson well understood from football. When it's time to return to their classrooms, the smallest ('foundation') children leave first. Then the infants and lastly the juniors line up and depart, having first put away their balls, hula hoops and other equipment.

The whole dinner hour programme has been very well thought out, and is clearly a big improvement. I thoroughly enjoyed my 'dinner date', and thank the staff and the children who looked after me so well and answered my many questions.

Proposed Alterations to the Primary & Secondary Schools (May 2007)

The Parish Council's Annual Report for 2006/2007 noted:

'The **Primary School** is to become an 'Integrated Children's Centre' along with 8 other schools in York. A development plan has been established alongside other interested parties (social services, health services etc.) in a bid to amalgamate all services into one building. Building is well under way.

The **Joseph Rowntree School** has been awarded £23.7 million to re-develop its site involving demolishing the existing building and re-building.

Plans have yet to be agreed upon. Some preparatory work will be necessary (archaeological) not only on the school site but also across the Old School Field. This is not intended to be a part of the new development but usage of the field for utility works that may have to cross the field. Councillor Crawford is a member of the core Development Group.'

Joseph Rowntree School and the Joseph Rowntree Trust – by Sally Shaw, one of the School Governors (August 2005)

This article is about how the long-standing link between our school and the Joseph Rowntree Trust benefits pupils and the local community.

Joseph Rowntree School is, like most state-funded secondary schools, an 11-18 co-educational comprehensive, catering for students of all abilities. However Joseph Rowntree School is unique amongst secondary schools in that it was founded in 1942 by the Joseph Rowntree Memorial Trust and became a Voluntary Controlled school. This means that as well as receiving exactly the same funding and support from the Local Education Authority as other schools, we benefit in addition from the special relationship we have with the Joseph Rowntree Foundation.

The school has always enjoyed a special relationship with the local community. Many adults in the York area remember with affection their time at the school. Today's students come mostly from the garden village of New Earswick, and the villages of Haxby, Wigginton and Strensall, although increasing numbers attend from within the City. The catchment area extends from Bootham Bar by York Minister to the countryside north of Haxby/Wigginton. We have a fully comprehensive intake. The children are valued equally and we have high expectations of all.

The school has close links with the Joseph Rowntree Housing Trust. Several years ago the Trust became involved in a national charity called Communities that Care (CtC). This initiative brought together a group of about 20 people closely involved with New Earswick such as key local residents, youth workers, staff from the Housing Trust and Mrs Wright, the Deputy Head of the secondary school. Communities that Care has enabled the school to work together with the Trust.

Five years ago the Trust commissioned researchers to conduct a survey of young people at secondary schools. Joseph Rowntree School took part in this research, which consisted of a lengthy questionnaire for students to find out their views about school life, home life, relationships, leisure interests etc. The findings revealed much information about the lives of young people in our communities and as a result a researcher was commissioned to attend CtC Board meetings. This research has led to discussions about highlighted 'risk factors' and collaborative thinking about how to target resources.

Recently, after five years, this questionnaire has been re-run for the same group of students and it will be interesting to learn how much has changed, in the lives of these young people, over five years.

The Trust has additional important influences upon the school's operation. For example five governors are nominated by the Joseph Rowntree Foundation. The governors devote much time and considerable effort to support the school and its aims. Additionally the

Foundation supports the existence of our outdoor activity centre at Stape, on the North Yorkshire Moors. This residential field centre is known as the Ken Ather Centre. Help from the Foundation has enabled the upgrading of the centre, which provides sleeping, work and recreational facilities for our students. (We have many teachers to thank for, without recompense (!), giving up much time to assist with the upgrade.) The upgrade has been of such a high standard that it is now possible to rent it out to other organisations to raise revenue for re-investing in further improvements.

Another initiative linking the school with work supported by the Trust is the 'Sleeper Path' Youth Project. Generous funding from the Trust paid for the renovation of old tractor sheds on the 'Sleeper Path'. Young people played a big part in working with the architects and builders from the Trust to plan the project. Deputy Head, Mrs Wright, was invited from the school to the opening of this facility and is now involved in placing students to take part in the 'Momentum on 2 Wheels' project run by the York Youth Service. Here young people have the opportunity to develop off-road motorbike riding skills, learn about basic motorbike maintenance and explore their own attitudes and responsibilities to being a bike user. Since the project started 4 groups from the Joseph Rowntree School have taken part, involving 31 young people. The students were rewarded and acknowledged in school for their achievements.

Recently the Trust has funded a specialist Youth Worker to mentor students. The Youth Worker provides an informal presence at lunchtime and builds relationships with students. Young people in need of additional support can gain great value from this service.

Other examples of invaluable assistance from the Trust include the recent purchase of new netball kit for our highly successful netball teams. The Trust also encourages and facilitates projects carried out by the school. It has enabled our artists to exhibit their work in the Folk Hall – an example being the 'litter' project, whereby litter was collected from around the village and transformed into artwork.

Last year, to commemorate the centenary of the village of New Earswick, the Trust invited students from the art department to produce and exhibit paintings of houses in the village. The project began with residents of New Earswick taking groups of students on guided tours of the village and culminated in an exhibition of artwork in the Folk Hall.

Joseph Rowntree School has a positive attitude to collaborating with other agencies and values our unique link with the Trust and the community of New Earswick.

Bunking Off   (January 2006)

It is among older pupils that 'unofficial' truanting is most common; they simply answer the register in the morning and then disappear, either missing particular lessons or bunking off for the day. A national survey of Year 11 students produced results showing how often they truanted. The range varies as follows: most frequently (i.e. between once a week and every day) it was 9.9%; for once to three times a month it was 12.3%; and it was 13.6% when it occurred less often. It is generally accepted that these figures do not reveal the full extent of the problem. The young people themselves completed the survey, so it has to be noted that the most persistent truants would not have been present to answer it.

This particular survey was conducted in 1993. Ten years and nearly one billion pounds later, we are now experiencing the biggest increase in truancy for years. A vivid picture emerges of 55,000 empty desks in schools in England, *every day*.

So, what is to be done about it? The Government's Fast Track Attendance Scheme proposes that parents are given 12 weeks in which to improve their child's attendance. After that time, they will be faced with a fine of £2,500 or three months in prison. Another initiative, Every Lesson Counts, adopts a 'carrot' rather than a 'stick' policy. The travel industry is to offer discounts and other incentives to encourage families to make early bookings for the school holiday periods.

These proposals would cover cases lasting weeks or months. But missing a day, or even one lesson, can mean missing some vital instruction, such as how electronic circuits depend on the binary system of counting, or the correct use of the apostrophe. (A surprisingly large number of people seem to have missed the latter!) It is the sort of thing which places the returning truant at a disadvantage in class, leading to teasing, then to bullying, and inevitably to a greater reluctance to attend school. Alternatively, their reaction may take the form of disruptive behaviour affecting the whole class, which may possibly result in exclusion. Whether the truant becomes a bully, or the victim of bullying, it's a wretched outcome.

It is pretty obvious that prevention is better than cure and there is no shortage of helpful suggestions from the academics. Numbered among them are electronic registration, and same-day response to any unauthorised absence. But being let off homework, as an incentive to attend school, would surely make the 'catching up' process even harder.

Just as individual pupils have varied conditions and needs, so do the schools they attend. Each school should be allowed to work out its own tactics for dealing with truancy. At the Joseph Rowntree School, attendance is recorded in the morning and again in the afternoon. Absentees from individual lessons are also noted. The first stage of an Attendance Challenge has recently been launched, aiming to improve attendance by 1% – just one and a half days over a five week period. There are prizes for tutor groups within each year, and there is a draw to reward those individuals who achieve full attendance and the most improved attendance. Besides being a habit well worth acquiring, good attendance promotes high achievement.

The Library   (March 2003)

New Earswick Library is thought to be the first village library in this area, having been established some time before 1920. The original stock of books was supplied by the Cocoa Works, as Rowntrees was then known. Given Joseph Rowntree's enthusiasm for self-help communities, it comes as no surprise that it was administered by the Village Council and a team of volunteers. The library itself was upstairs in the Folk Hall. This area has since been divided to form the office

From the original architect's drawing for the new library.

annexe, with a further small room beyond the glass partition.

So when the new custom-built library was opened in 1975 with a total floor space of over 140 square metres, it represented a considerable expansion. There are about 7,000 books, organised into a children's section, an adults' section and a small collection of reference books, plus a range of electronic gadgetry available for public use. The computer system has recently been updated; its facilities include word processing and access to the internet. There is a scanner and a printer which can produce black and white or colour copies; all the user has to pay for is the printing.

As to the books themselves, the number issued on loan has doubled over the last two years (2001/3), particularly to the younger age groups. No doubt they have been encouraged to use the library by the introduction of a reading club and a colouring club.

The earliest users of lending libraries, the monks, would be amazed to see how the service has advanced since the days when it was a privilege to be allowed to borrow books from the monastery library. Today, *we* would be amazed if, like, the monks, we had to prove that we had read the books we had borrowed!

Public libraries really came into their own when it became possible to publish books at a selling price of a shilling (5p) or even half that, with the advent of steam to power the printing presses. By 1800, there were about a hundred libraries in London and a thousand in other parts of the country. Novels and other light reading became extremely popular, in addition to DIY and Teach Yourself books. Even before Mrs Beeton, Hannah Glasse published *The Art of Cookery Made Plain and*

Easy in 1747. This was written for servants so as to 'save the Ladies a great deal of Trouble'!

At around the same time, children's books were being produced, but children's sections did not feature in lending libraries until the second half of the 19th century. Until then, books were issued to children by request only, from a catalogue. There was no means whereby young readers could browse the shelves.

It was a Yorkshire woman, Eileen Colwell, who helped to change all that. Born in 1904, she was taken by her father to buy a Nelson Sixpenny Classic every week, from the age of seven. When she was 17, she won a scholarship to study Librarianship at University College London, and never looked back.

At the age of 22, she moved to Hendon, where she had obtained a part-time temporary post as a librarian. But there was no public library! So she set up a service for children, which operated in the evenings from local schools. To start off, she was given several hundred books by Foyle's. That first year, there were 25,000 issues, and this was doubled the following year. Eventually she had a network of 14 schools being used as evening libraries for children. Furthermore, she trained the children to help with issuing books; she taught them how to use the catalogue and encouraged them to write book reviews.

By 1937 she had set up the Association of Children's Libraries. Its aim was the creation of attractive and welcoming areas in public libraries, all over the country. They were designed to stock a wide selection of books of interest to children.

As a result, the local library is now the place where a toddler can listen to stories, and where a scholar can carry out research. The rest of us have access to a wide range of books to take home and read at leisure; for 'a home without books is like a house without windows.'

Book Reviews – by John and Enid Harrington (October 2003)

We had only lived in York for a short time when we saw the appeal for book reviewers in the *New Earswick Bulletin*. In those days, like Shakespeare's *Cleopatra*, we were 'tender in heart and green in experience' so we volunteered.

As we collected and reviewed our first two books we began to have some qualms about what we might have taken on but when the reviews appeared in print we were reassured. We received many compliments and expressions of interest. People continue to tell us how they look forward to our contributions. The librarian was warmly appreciative and we understand there has been an increase in requests for books which have been reviewed – a very happy outcome.

One question which is often asked is, 'How do you choose the books to be reviewed?' The answer is that they are selected for us by the librarian. We prefer this arrangement as it helps us to be objective and gives us an incentive to consider the merits of books which have no initial appeal for us. An unforgettable example was *Go*, a frenetic tale about violent drug-fuelled layabouts. Some people might enjoy it so it was our responsibility to review it dispassionately.

Most of the books have been more conventional in style but they have covered an enormous range of fact and fiction from a fantasy about gun-toting fairies (*Artemis Fowl*) to a guide to the library services in the City of York.

From month to month each of us tries to vary the kind of book which we review. So far the choosing process has not led to any marital discord and we have not had to toss a coin or draw lots. If we did, the loser would probably get a book which had won an award or been acclaimed by literary critics!

The views expressed in the reviews are entirely our own. The only requirements are to review the book within the normal three-week borrowing period, to keep the written submission to about 200 words and not to reveal the ending of any work of fiction. Books come between covers and on tape. With experience it is fairly easy to trace the storyline of a printed book by sampling. An audio-book, however, must be heard from beginning to end even if it is a history of the Land Army in twelve instalments!

Most of the books we have reviewed have been interesting and entertaining. Some have given us new perspectives. *No Drinking, No Doctors, No Dancing* gave a thoughtful interpretation of the overworked theme of an Irish childhood. *Unless*, with its feminine insights, converted its male reviewer to the work of Carol Shields.

To date we have not reviewed any children's books. Perhaps these are best left to the age-group for which they are intended. The *New Earswick Bulletin* has featured one review by a ten-year-old girl, and this is something to be encouraged. It would also be reassuring to know that, when we handed in our final borrowing slips, there would be someone to carry on this rewarding activity.

Keeping New Earswick Tidy (October 2003)

How many litter bins would you say there are in New Earswick? Counting those along the various walks, as well as the roads and snickets, the total comes to 26. You would think that would be enough, but there is still a need for the Cleansing Partnership to keep an eye on it all.

The partners include the Joseph Rowntree Housing Trust, in whose ownership much of New Earswick lies, the New Earswick Residents' Forum, and the Parish Council. Over all, is the City of York Council, in the shape of the Environmental and Development Services and the Cleansing Services. Once a month, representatives from all these bodies meet to discuss the problems and decide what can be done about them. Weather permitting, they go on a litter walk to see for themselves.

While many of us are still having breakfast, John Ward (CoYC) is out and about, emptying the bins and tidying the area in front of the shops. That's the time New Earswick looks its cleanest. Then the schoolchildren, commuters and shoppers come along and start the daily litter drop. It seems to begin with fag ends – I counted 48 one morning in the bus shelter outside the secondary school. At lunch time, fish and chip boxes, crisp bags, sweet wrappers, and empty soft drink cans and bottles make their appearance, especially along the route from the secondary school to the shops, via Chestnut Grove and Sycamore Avenue. (A new bin has recently been installed on the corner there.)

Presumably the same sort of scene confronts John Ward when he moves on to the other areas under his care – Huntington, Haxby, Wigginton, Strensall, Skelton and Rawcliffe.

Litter on the pavements and in the bus shelters is easy enough sweep up, but living in a garden village like New

Earswick means there are miles of hedgerow, so litter lodges in the hedge bottoms, and plastic bags catch on the thorns. If the litter lies on the householder's side of the hedge, then he or she has to clear it away, even though it's been thrown, (or blown) there. If it's on the public side, then it's the responsibility of the various public services.

A new system is being tried out, whereby Michael Sawyer (JRHT) will check the numerous snickets whenever he can fit this in with his other work. By the time you read this, the Cleansing Partnership will have noted any improvements.

As for the areas around the library, behind the swimming baths and along the path leading past the tennis club to Red Lodge, these are kept tidy by Jason O'Dwyer, also of the JRHT staff. His responsibilities include the state of the youth shelter, and recently he had to paint over the graffiti on its outer walls. Not for the last time, I suspect! Another new litter bin has been placed just outside this shelter.

The litter bins along the main highways are owned, supplied and maintained by the City of York Council. Extra ones for the Folk Hall bus shelter and the library area have been purchased by the Parish Council, which was then re-funded by the Joseph Rowntree Housing Trust.

Another approach is through the Ward Committee, but this can be a lengthy process. Their public meetings are held only once a quarter (whereas the Parish Council meets on a monthly basis). First a bid has to be made; then all the ward residents have to be given the opportunity to 'express a preference' and that means those from Huntington as well as New Earswick. The actual decision is made later by the three Ward Committee Councillors.

A bid from New Earswick for two bins proved successful and the sum of £1320 was allocated. But the next step, installing the bins, took more than six months: a 'ridiculous time scale' in the opinion of our Parish Council.

The Cleansing Partnership, on the other hand, is a good example of effective co-operation providing the service we need; for it seems that litter, like the poor, will always be with us.

A glance at the floor of the youth shelter or any of our bus shelters shows that people are too lazy to use litter bins placed less than a metre away.

The amenities listed below are briefly described in a recent (2007) report by Social Regeneration Consultants:

'The Swimming Pool is also centrally located. The pool was built in 1967 and at the time was seen to be adequate; however, it is now seen as 'outdated', but a much-appreciated and heavily used facility.

The facility has a 20 metre pool, with male and female changing rooms. The pool is used by the New Earswick Swimming Club. The Swimming Club has a large number of members who mainly live in New Earswick, Haxby and Huntington. The club is split into two groups; recreational swimming and competitive swimming and training. The local community can hire the swimming pool for birthday parties or other events.

The **play facilities** in the centre of New Earswick next to the Swimming Pool and Library include a children's play area, basketball court and a multi-purpose grassed area with goal posts.

The Tennis Courts are used by the New Earswick Tennis Club. There are three courts and a clubhouse which provides changing rooms, a small kitchen and communal area. The club has 30 adult members and 30 junior members. Only two adult members are from the village, though a higher proportion of the junior members are from the village.'

Flood protection: In January 2001, the following letter about the culverting of Westfield Beck was received from Peter Giles, Deputy Director of Housing Property Services, Joseph Rowntree Housing Trust:

Much of the flooding that used to occur in New Earswick was due to Westfield Beck. In order to reduce the risk of this happening, a number of things have been done:

The beck is culverted within large diameter pipes for much of its route through the village. The volume of water in the beck, as it passes through New Earswick is controlled by sluice gates in the field where Hartrigg Oaks has been built. A pumping station (owned by Yorkshire Water) pumps any excess floodwater from the beck to the River Foss via a large diameter underground pipe.

Surface water drainage from the new housing built in the village and from the newly constructed roads, throughout the older part of New Earswick, goes into drainage pipes that discharge into the into the River Foss south of the village. The level of water in the River Foss is controlled by pumps situated at the Foss Basin where it joins the River Ouse. This reduces the risk of flooding to properties adjacent to the River Foss.

We wish to confirm that during the recent record flood levels (in 2000), on all rivers in the area, we had no major problems in New Earswick. Properties alongside the River Foss such as Lock Cottage, Petland and

Sleeper Track Youth Club were protected by sandbags as a precaution, but fortunately the river did not rise to these levels.

Westfield Beck as it emerges from the culverts below Western Terrace.

CHAPTER FIVE

The Parish Council

Three Score Years and Ten (May 2004)

It was seventy years ago, on 14 April 1934, that New Earswick Parish Council held its first meeting. Before that it was one parish with Huntington and both were part of Flaxton Rural District.

What are the deciding factors in the creation of a parish council? They have been set out very clearly in a recent government circular. Parish councils have two main roles, community representation and local representation; therefore 'for both purposes it is desirable that a parish should reflect a small, distinctive and recognisable community of interest, with its own sense of identity.'

At that first parish council meeting, Mr James W. Hallaways was elected chairman. He stressed the good relationship which had always existed between the two sides of the parish (New Earswick and Huntington) and expressed the wish that these would continue. There were, and still are, a number of matters of joint concern. One of them was the maintenance of the Foss which at that time was considered to be in a serious condition. This was before the Ministry of Agriculture established the Foss Catchment Board (now the Foss Drainage Board) and the Foss was a shared responsibility. Why was this so? Because under the mapping conventions, those parish boundaries which follow a river are plotted along its centre.

In fact the state of the banks of the River Foss came up for discussion at that first meeting. York City Council disclaimed all responsibility for their maintenance, as they had done repeatedly in the past, but promised to make enquiries. Mr Hallaways reminded councillors that the City Council had on two occasions compensated landowners for damage due to floods resulting from the poor condition of the banks. So it was decided to ask Flaxton for advice on the legal position.

Flaxton Rural District Council was also to be asked for advice about the condition of the ditch along the west bank of the Foss. The Joseph Rowntree Village Trust considered that the condition of the ditch was none of their business. So the 'stagnant and offensive' water, unable to get away from the very deep channel adjoining Church Lane, remained a recurring problem.

The division of the former large parish and a change in York City boundaries meant that the York Gas Company had to be informed about the disposition of the street lamps. Mapping of all known footpaths had to be recorded for future reference and again both were done in co-operation with Huntington.

That was quite a full agenda with much follow-up work to be done, so it was decided ('after some discussion') that a clerk to the council should be appointed. A sub-committee of three was asked to advertise the post, interview applicants, and appoint a suitable person. At the following meeting, the appointment of Mr W.E. Williams of 30 Hawthorn Terrace was confirmed, at a commencing salary of £5 per annum. One of his first duties was to purchase a Minute Book and other necessary stationery. He was later authorised to buy a handbook dealing with the powers of parish councils.

The first Minute Book spans the years from 1934 to 1938. Much of the detail is routine, but there are some fascinating nuggets of information in those handwritten records. What is missing, of course, is details about the first ten parish councillors. One of them was Mrs Edith Marion Waind, who became chairman of the council when Mr Hallaways died in the summer of 1936. I have recently discovered that York City library has a card-index system with references to newspaper items about local people. Thus it was, that in checking the spelling of Mrs Waind's name (a new one to me and I wanted to get it right), I discovered that she lived at West Croft, New Earswick, and was headmistress of Park Grove Junior School for 11 years. Her husband, Lt. Arthur Waind, had been killed in World War I shortly after their marriage. She died in 1941.

New Earswick Parish Council's first Minute Book.

All Saints Churchyard – from Parish Council Notes (December 2002)

A meeting with councillors from Earswick, New Earswick and Huntington was attended to discuss the way forward with the repairs required to this closed churchyard. A risk assessment report has been carried out by Dossor Taylors, which details the need for immediate repairs to the boundary wall, and some headstones are dangerously unstable. It was agreed the wall be rebuilt as soon as possible and the invoice be divided in the usual proportions (i.e. Huntington 75%, New Earswick 20% and Earswick 5%). This is an unexpected cost to this council this year but a very necessary one to safeguard users of the church.

Regarding the headstones, it was agreed that an effort would be made to contact relatives to inform them of their dangerous condition. It was agreed an advert in the local press and notices posted on all usual notice boards around the 3 parishes would suffice. This would detail the requirements as stated in the risk assessment report to lay the stones down. Failing in a response, the stone would be laid down in a respectful and proper manner.

A joint application will be made to our Ward Committee for a grant towards these necessary repairs.

Resting in Peace   (March 2005)

In 1982, the graveyard at All Saints' Church was approaching full capacity. It was (and still is) the responsibility of the parishes of Earswick, New Earswick and Huntington; since the need to find a new site had become critical, a Burial Board was established with representatives from the three parish councils. Councillors Cawood, Crossling and Snowdon represented New Earswick, Huntington had five Board members and there were two from Earswick. This ratio of three, five and two reflected the relative sizes of their populations.

As far as New Earswick's Board members were concerned, Mr Crossling had to resign quite early on, because of ill-health. He was replaced by Councillor K. Robinson. After the death of Mr Snowdon, Mrs Ellis was appointed to the Burial Board; Miss Cawood remained a Board member until her resignation from New Earswick Parish Council in 2003, after almost 24 years as a councillor.

When the Board began its work, two sites were under consideration, both part of Mr Bowling's farm: a triangle to the north of Huntington churchyard and a rectangle to the west. Either would, in effect, be an extension of the graveyard. Ryedale District Council, to which the three parishes then belonged, had granted planning permission for the two sites. Which one was it to be, and would a compulsory purchase order be necessary?

At a site meeting in August 1982, such matters as the need for levelling off, drainage, fencing, provision of a water supply, and the erection of a permanent building were all considered. Access, especially for the necessary mechanical equipment to do the work, was also discussed.

In December the Board received a report on the inquiry into the land purchase and it was decided to find out if the triangle of land was still on the market and to ask the Water Authority to carry out a survey. Following this, they would need to know drainage costs and also the depth of the water table (for the purpose of digging double graves). As a result of the report, the Board decided to offer £400. Mr Bowling attended the next meeting at which there was a long discussion on the state and quality of the land and whether a more realistic price was between £750 and £1,000. In view of this difference, it is hardly surprising that at its next meeting the Board decided to ask Ryedale District Council officers to seek a piece of land elsewhere.

The same procedure had to be followed all over again for the land they eventually found in New Lane. It was not until December 1986, nearly five years after their initial meeting, that the site became the Board's property at a cost of £14,000, New Earswick's share being £2,833. Just as they were probably breathing a collective sigh of relief, they were informed that North Yorkshire County Council wanted one third of the land for a new road! They immediately voted to negotiate for land as compensation, rather than money. At a later meeting Mr Cudworth (Chief Executive of RDC) agreed to make a 'vigorous approach' to the County Council regarding a proposed exchange of some land belonging to Miss Cass of North Lane as a solution. Just as this proposal was reaching a conclusion, another snag arose in the form of

a planned roundabout from the superstore at Monks Cross. Fortunately, a developer showed an interest in exchanging land for a field in New Lane and this proved to be the answer.

During the six years it took to find a site, the Board had been planning the layout of grave plots and flagged pathways, road access and parking. Now, at last, they could go ahead. The design for the gates was approved; trees were ordered from Castle Howard and hedges were planted. A cabin for storage purposes was erected, water was laid on and bins were provided for dead flowers and wreaths.

The Bishop of Selby was asked to dedicate the ground on 8 September 1988.

Now, some 16 years later, visitors to the cemetery find a green and peaceful place. Gravestones are placed head to head, to allow easy access from the paths and there are seats where one may spend time in quiet contemplation.

There seems to be considerable freedom in the wording of epitaphs and what kind of tributes are placed on the graves. Though not perhaps to everyone's taste, they are a moving testimony to deeply felt loss.

Rights of Way (June 2005)

New Earswick has an abundant choice of public footpaths, as long or as short as you like. They are clearly shown on the sketch map published by the Parish Council in 2003. It includes attractive photographs and informative descriptions to encourage us to explore our immediate surroundings. The map is on display on the Parish Council notice board outside the Happy Shopper, the

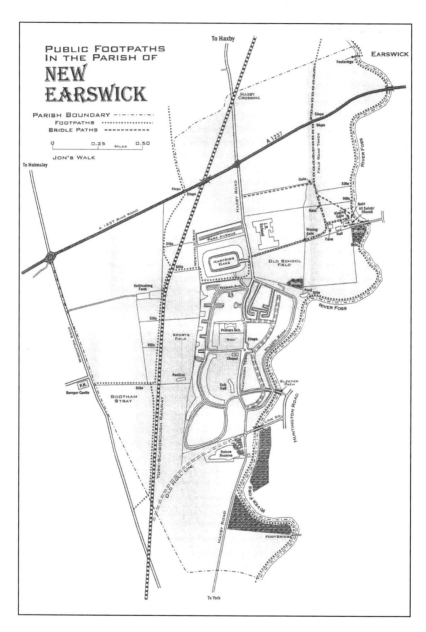

The Parish Council's sketch map, 2003.

Post Office, the Library and the Folk Hall. All 10 km of them are rights of way, with just one exception. That is Jon's Walk in the south of the village. Jon Barker-Wyatt was the Deputy Director of Housing for the Joseph Rowntree Housing Trust, and when he died it was decided to create a path in his memory. It is for public use by courtesy of the Trust.

The other footpaths and the bridleway come under the wing of the Parish Council, some of whose members inspect them once a year, after which any maintenance requirements are reported to the Rights of Way Officer for the City of York Council. To avoid any confusion as to what needs doing and where, each path has a number. (All parishes were required to number their public rights of way under an Act of Parliament passed in 1949.)

There are two other groups of people who have responsibilities for rights of way. One is the general public. The Country Code (listed on the back of the New Earswick leaflet) tells us how best to 'enjoy the countryside and respect its life and work.' It's mostly common sense, but it's a useful reminder for adults and a handy summary for teaching the younger generation. For fuller explanations the Countryside Agency's book *Out in the Country* is very good. For example, it informs the reader that when you walk into a field 'sheep and lambs may run away, but cows and heifers are naturally inquisitive and may follow you.' Hence the need to move carefully and quietly and to keep your dog under control.

The third group of people who are involved in managing the network of footpaths are landowners and farmers. Their particular duty is to keep the rights of way clear. In the past, various complaints have been made to the Parish Council on this score. One was that the footpath to Wigginton had been ploughed up. The farmer is allowed to do this if the path crosses the middle of the field, but he must restore the route within a maximum of 14 days.

Other problems may not be so easy to solve, such as a bull being turned into a field over which there is a right of way. When, in 1941, the Parish Council investigated a complaint about a bull, members of the Footpaths Sub-Committee were unable to establish the facts. The bull had gone – if indeed it was ever there.

Responsibility for the condition of stiles, gates and footbridges lies with the local authority. Recently, new stiles were constructed by volunteers from the Parish Paths Partnership. This was a joint initiative between parish councils, local interest groups, the City of York Council and the Countryside Commission. Furthermore all the rights of way were signposted and waymarked with yellow arrows. An exception is our one bridleway which runs east from Haxby Road Farm; it has a blue arrow.

Some of our rights of way have been incorporated into long distance walks, like the Millennium Way and the Centenary Way. The Millennium Way is the most recent and is a 23-mile walk which enters New Earswick along the Foss Way and goes as far north as All Saints Church. It then branches off to the west past the Joseph Rowntree School, crosses the main Haxby road, skirts round Hartrigg Oaks and turns south at the railway line to Bootham Stray, and so back to York.

Centenary Way was developed by the County Council to celebrate its hundredth anniversary in 1989. It makes

Millennium Way signpost.

use of the Foss Way as a route through New Earswick. In the north east corner of our parish, it crosses the footbridge into Earswick in order to complete the whole walk from York Minster to Filey.

So – one 'way' or another we have plenty of choice!

Rights of Way Walk – by Richard Revell, Member of New Earswick Parish Council and its Rights of Way Officer, from *Hartrigg Oaks News* (June 2002)

Councillor Crawford and I met just before 10.00 a.m. at Park Lodge on Sunday 23 July – a warm summer morning. After waiting till five past ten in case anyone else should join us, we decided to stay as a single group, rather than split in two, and set off to inspect the walk from Park Lodge to Bumper Castle on Wigginton Road. Back at the end of May parts of this walk were very difficult and waterlogged, especially the section from the railway line to Wigginton Road.

We walked down the side of Hartrigg Oaks and over Westfield Beck. At the stile leading into the field before the railway line we discovered the gate-post had been replaced and the old wooden one, which had the yellow way-marker arrow attached, was lying in the bushes nearby. There was a crop growing in the field, but the farmer had correctly left the path clear from the stile across to the railway line.

After carefully crossing the railway tracks we turned left and followed the path across the fields and over two stiles alongside the railway line, and then turned right towards Bumper Castle. Fortunately for us, the path was no longer waterlogged, although it was very uneven in places under the flattened grass, and some of the bushes on either side require cutting back. After a short halt at Wigginton Road (not Bumper Castle itself!) we retraced our steps as far as Hartrigg Oaks. Following a few words with a resident in one of Rowan Avenue's back gardens, we went our separate ways. It had been an enjoyable one-and-a-half hour stroll in pleasant surroundings and good company.

A Tall Story   (June 2002)

Let's get one thing straight from the start: this is the telecommunications tower which has been standing in a field at Crompton Farm for the last year or so. And another thing we need to get clear is that Crompton Farm *is* in New Earswick. Take no notice of the HAXBY sign on the millwheel just over the ring road – the northern boundary of New Earswick is actually the railway line, not the A1237. So that means the telecommunications tower, which belongs to Orange plc, *is* our business.

We have to go back two years, to the middle of May 2000, when Orange first applied for planning permission to build a telecommunications tower. Originally they wanted to erect it at the Telephone Exchange in Park Avenue. It would have been 22.5 metres high, with 18 antennae, four dishes, an equipment cabin, a meter cabinet and security fencing.

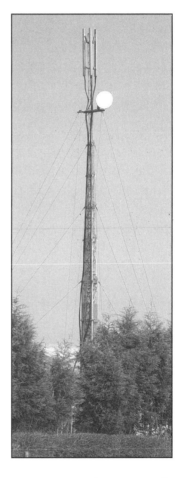

Considering its position, on the corner of Park Avenue and Park Terrace, and opposite the Joseph Rowntree School, the Parish Council advised strongly against it. They were particularly concerned about recent reports of the effects of radiation emissions on young people. In addition to that, they thought the visual impact on the surrounding Green Belt land was unacceptable. A further factor was its proximity to neighbouring gardens and to the school.

The City of York Council took the advice of the Parish Council, and planning permission was refused. Orange then had the bright idea of erecting a temporary pole.

This meant that since it was less than 15 metres tall, it did not need planning permission at that time. And there it has stood, next to three poplar trees and a field which is often full of sheep, at Crompton Farm.

Of course Orange soon wanted to replace the temporary structure with a permanent one, and so they applied for permission to erect a telecommunications monopole – 20 metres high this time. It was to have two microwave dishes and six dual polar antennae, the equipment cabin, meter cabinet and security fencing. The Parish Council could see that this might be 'the thin end of the wedge' with scope for the addition of more antennae at a later date.

Five residents from Crompton Terrace came to a meeting of the Parish Council where they voiced their objections. Councillors took a keen interest in the problem, asking many questions. They then voted unanimously against the application and their comments were forwarded to the City of York Council. These were that there was still no proof that the emissions are not harmful; local residents were very concerned about the effects on their own health, that of nearby schoolchildren and on farm and domestic animals. There was noise pollution from the audible alarm system, which could possibly go on and on – after all, the station was unmanned and a night-time response could take a long time. The siting of the monopole (hardly a thing of beauty) was still within the Green Belt area and would have a visual impact for miles around, as has been the case with the shorter, temporary structure.

By February of last year, the Chairman of the Parish Council had attended a planning meeting of the City Council and been interviewed by Radio York. In March he was able to report that Orange had withdrawn its application.

Then followed a delay due to the outbreak of foot and mouth disease, which meant that access to the fields to find an alternative site was denied. Eventually, Orange found a suitable place: still on Crompton Farm, but well away from any dwellings and in a field where there are already a good number of pylons. If you drive east along the A1237, the site is on the left hand side of the road, opposite the pumping station. And this – at long last – was acceptable.

Parish Emergency Plan – from Parish Council Notes (June 2005)

City of York Council is assisting this Council in establishing a parish plan. It details requirements for a specific parish relating to all types of emergencies (e.g. flooding, accidents on the ring-road involving toxic spillage, gas leaks, disaster and evacuation conditions, severe weather conditions etc.) and who or what action we would need to take should these situations arise within this parish. We will invite partners in the parish to assist in formulating a plan and form a conduit structure into the emergency services with the emphasis on protocols to be observed.

It will take the form of a comprehensive register of up-to-date valuable local information and conditions, which would greatly assist the emergency services. Of course emergency plans already exist for every community. The PEP is to customise the details to the requirements of the parish of New Earswick.

A working group has been set up to co-ordinate all information required consisting of Councillors Crawford,

Hudson and Alley, the Clerk, Peter Giles (JRHT) and Barry Kelly from CoYC.

Where Charity Begins   (June 2006)

Parish councils have the power to spend money on charitable giving, and they do this through the precept. Although the precept is collected along with the council tax payment by the City of York, the amount is set by parish council members and it is they who decide how it should be spent.

Because a large part of New Earswick is owned and administered by the Joseph Rowntree Housing Trust, our Parish Council has fewer responsibilities than most. But, as with all parish councils, it remains the least bureaucratic kind of local authority. It is also the cheapest because the councillors work voluntarily. Nine of the ten members actually live within New Earswick (the qualifying limit is within three miles) and all are in close touch with the affairs of the parish.

The maximum amount allowed by legislation for charitable giving is calculated on the basis of £5 per head of the electorate.   It must be distributed as the Parish Council wishes, but not all to a single organisation or person.

Some of the donations appear regularly in the annual accounts, for instance the Summer Scheme, the Gardening Scheme and the Royal British Legion Poppy appeal.   For each one, members discuss the amount to be given and whether or not there should be an increase. They are guided by the rate of inflation or by an awareness of a particular need. The Summer Scheme, which operates for the four middle weeks of the long summer holiday and provides organised activities for youngsters from 12 to 17 years of age, was felt to be so important that councillors voted to double the contribution for this year. (Council regulations demand that a formal vote be taken on all matters of finance.)

The project or activity concerned must be one where the majority of participants are from the parish of New Earswick itself, although it may be open to people from surrounding areas, *e.g.* the Junior Angling Club at the Nature Reserve. Secondly, it must be for a specific purpose, and if it is not spent for that purpose, the Council requires the money to be returned.

A bench beside the Old School Playing Field, donated by the Parish Council.

Thirdly, council members like to know that fund-raising efforts have already been made. A good example is the Church Lads' and Church Girls' Brigade, who give concerts to pay for musical instruments. Another is the New Earswick Indoor Bowls Club. They needed an electronic scoreboard, and the council contributed towards its cost. The Club's annual Bring and Buy Sale is a triumph of organisation and hard work; prior to the event, advice is taken on goods of particular value so that they realise a fair price. After the sale, the left-overs are taken to a car boot sale.

Assistance has recently been given to the Methodist Church for alterations to improve disabled access. Its members run a Christmas Fayre and they sell home-made jam and cakes throughout the year.

A special gift commemorating the Parish Council's 70th anniversary has been the new gates at the primary school. The design has involved the school governors, the staff and the children as well as the Parish Council.

Charitable giving is only part of Parish Council work but it is no wonder their annual report states 'This council is delighted to have been able to offer support to ...'

The new gates at the Primary School, commemorating the Parish Council's 70th Anniversary.

New Council Office – from Parish Council Notes (April 2005)

A budget to purchase new equipment (desk, filing cabinets etc.) was agreed at £700. The agreement for the rental of the office was signed by the Chairman on behalf of the Council and returned to NECA.

The new phone line should be working on 16 May 2005 and should transfer the existing number over from the Clerk's home. The line at the Clerk's house will then cease. There may be an unavoidable break in service regarding the Internet for the Council but emails can be accessed from other computers using specific AOL passwords. The Clerk will investigate the possibility of a new server (cheaper) for the Internet.

The Ward Committee: a New Approach (April 2005)

You have to hand it to the Ward Committee: they do keep trying to attract reluctant residents to their meetings. Last time it was a Community Fayre, as reported in the June-July issue of the *Bulletin*. This time they tried a 'map-building' exercise, which had been very well-planned and deserved a much better attendance than about thirty people.

First we had an opportunity to meet our two new Ward Committee members, as well as our own Parish Councillors. Then, after half an hour of chit chat and refreshments, we were set to work on the map-building. Four large scale maps of the ward, about 6 ft. by 4 ft., had been spread out on tables, each one having a different theme. The idea was for us to write our ideas on post-it notes and stick them on the appropriate part of the map, to identify the hot spots.

Each table was attended by someone to answer questions and I think this gave more satisfaction to those present than the map-building. For example Peter Giles from the Joseph Rowntree Housing Trust was kept very busy discussing break-ins and vandalism at the Crime and Community Safety table. Also in attendance at this table were our new Ward Manager (PC Paul Beckwith) plus a couple of representatives from Mayfair Security; Richard York was there too, on behalf of the New Earswick Residents' Forum, and the New Earswick Police Consultative Group.

By the end of the meeting all four maps showed a fair sprinkling of post-it notes. The Environment included the state of the roads and verges, as well as recycling and composting. Community and Youth issues revealed a wish for more activities for young people and for the over-fifties. (Presumably those in the intermediate age groups already have quite enough to do!) Transport and Road Safety brought out the problem of cycles on footpaths and the need for designated cycle lanes.

As residents of New Earswick know very well, these subjects can't be treated in isolation. Satan certainly finds mischief for idle hands to do and so we see young people breaking almost every road safety rule, vandalising the environment, and indulging in petty crime.

> 'If young adolescents don't have a place of their own to go to, it may increase the risk of minor damage that can take place when they meet in unsuitable places, which can lead to a spiral of anti-social behaviour and the start of a criminal record.'

This extract is from the *Newsletter of the York and North Yorkshire Playing Fields Association* (Spring 2003). The report goes on to say that what the young people need is somewhere where they can meet their friends, without adult supervision. Calling such a place a 'chat room' rather than a youth shelter, the report (from the Thames Valley Police) recommends a vandal-resistant framework of structural steel, with a high density black polythene roof. The resulting silver and black colour scheme has turned out to be very popular with the young. Though using these materials doesn't entirely eliminate graffiti, it can easily be removed. But would such a modern structure be acceptable in a conservation area?

Location is another factor: certainly not 'at the bottom of the playing field, miles from anything.' At this stage in their lives, many young people want to show off, especially to their peers. They need to be *seen* to be daring, clever, funny, or whatever.

This accounts for two recent incidents in New Earswick. One was the removal of roof tiles from the bus shelter opposite the shops at four o'clock in the afternoon. The other was the case of a young lad strutting along the flat roof of the garages adjoining the Old School Playing Field – also just as afternoon school was finishing.

A much more welcome sight was noticed on the way to the map-building meeting. Dozens of primary school children, accompanied by assorted adults, were walking, skipping and running along the footpath. They were having a whale of a time doing a treasure hunt. Long may such enjoyment continue and congratulations to everyone concerned!

CHAPTER SIX

Opportunities and Initiatives

A Community that Cares   (January 2004)

Communities that Care is an idea which originated in the United States and is now spreading to this country. It is a prevention programme aimed at 'unlocking the hidden strengths and potential that exist in every neighbourhood to build strong positive relationships between children and the individuals and institutions that are most likely to influence their development.'

New Earswick took its first steps towards becoming a Community that Cares in March of last year, and decided that its priorities were to improve youth provision and prevent truancy. The progress made in just under a year was described as 'impressive and exciting' by the CtC director for England when he attended the most recent meeting at The Garth.

Thanks to the backing of the Joseph Rowntree Housing Trust, New Earswick's CtC has been able to bring together projects which were already established, decide how best to support them and to identify other needs. An example of the former is the plan to boost numbers attending the football sessions. These are now held at the primary school, and it is hoped to increase participation to about 20. Already, two parents are involved in this. The Sleeper Path project also hopes for greater numbers: 40 per week, each young person attending sessions of two to three hours.

A reading group for 8 - 12 year-olds is currently in place at the library and there are workshops for the older age group. In this connection, New Earswick's Youth Worker (Victoria Dias) and Joy Cann, our librarian, are working together. Furthermore, Joy is now a volunteer member of the Youth Offenders Panel, which provides an opportunity for the offender, his or her parents, and the victim to meet together and discuss the best way forward. Future Prospects also makes use of the library for occasional Information Technology sessions. There are plans to develop these into a programme.

One of the most important agencies is of course the New Earswick Community Association which is in a position to provide premises at the Folk Hall, equipment and some funding, though naturally there is a limit. The Summer Scheme has already proved its worth; New Earswick Parish Council contributes to this each year. There are plans to increase the use of the Snooker Club, particularly by young women, and to establish a Junior Youth Club. A fortnightly Film Club which started in October also meets at the Folk Hall.

There is no shortage of ideas – only of volunteer supervisors. To the delight of all present at the recent CtC board meeting, one member volunteered there and then to supervise an arts and craft activity.

In addition, CtC wants to develop a system of rewarding those young people who do have responsible attitudes and who are willing to put something into the community. After all, why should only the disaffected youth receive all the attention? Ideas such as helping in the library and removing graffiti have been suggested, as have assistance with the recycling of compost and helping the old, the young and the housebound in various ways.

Last September, a discussion paper entitled 'What about the good kids?' – and there are plenty of them – was the subject of a meeting at which the bright ideas came thick and fast. Attention was given to ways of rewarding community work. What kind of tasks might be suitable, and how to assess their usefulness on a points system, still has to be thought through. This is a ground-breaking scheme, and it will involve some necessary supervision and record keeping.

Since coming to live in New Earswick I have been impressed by the happy recollections of older residents of their childhood days in the village. It was obviously a community that cared. Perhaps these new initiatives will ensure that today's young people will have equally happy memories.

Beginning at the Beginning (October 2005)

Education is recognised as a lifelong process, but until recently the emphasis has been on schools and further education, both formal and non-formal. Indeed, Joseph Rowntree himself took a great interest in adult education. Now, however, the pendulum is swinging to early education: education in the first few years of life, beginning soon after birth.

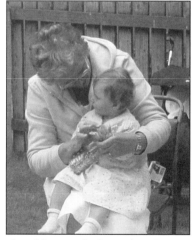

Peter Silva came to New Earswick just over a year ago to talk about a programme developed by his team in south-east Oxford. He said that the Peers High School in that area had found that:

'pupils leaving the high school were not able to compete fairly for jobs and further education as they had not managed to reach a competitive standard. This showed particularly in their literacy and numeracy.

The question was asked as to why they had not reached such a competitive standard, to which the answer came that they were too far behind when they came into the high school to catch up by the time they left. The same was said by the middle schools about why the pupils were behind when they arrived at the high school. And again,  the same was said by the first schools about why the pupils were behind when they arrived at the middle schools.

The conclusion then was to work with the children before they got to school so that they started at a level which enabled them to keep up with what was required of them by the schools. This meant working with the parents and carers who supported the children every day, all day. So that was how PEEP began.'

PEEP? It stands for **P**eers (after the high school which gave rise to this initiative) **E**arly **E**ducation **P**artnership, and it is the *partnership* between trained practitioners, parents and carers which is unique. Because partnership lies at the heart of Communities that Care, the New Earswick board decided to arrange for Rebecca Hill (Family Worker with the Joseph Rowntree Housing Trust), Wendy Lancaster (Health Visitor) and Clare Davenport (Little Rowans Early Years) to visit PEEP in action and to report back to the next board meeting.

As a result, the New Earswick PEEP was launched with a training session in March of this year. Eleven people attended the course and the babies group (open to all babies living in New Earswick) began on 12 April. On 19 July they held an open afternoon to celebrate the completion of the first term and to present certificates.

It was a charming occasion, beginning with a welcome

song which greets each person by name. Then there were more songs (PEEP has produced its own book of about 80 songs), followed by stories and a 'treasure chest' of everyday objects for the children to explore.

This, most people would say, is regular nursery school activity. But PEEP takes it further, with training carers in four ways. First is learning how to give the babies and young children the opportunity to do things, and second is to recognise and praise when they have learned something new. Third is the encouragement by interaction: doing things together (e.g. posting a letter), and last, being an example to the child. The latter was clearly demonstrated in the group 'sing-song': the babies listened and watched as the adults sang such numbers as *Intsy Wintsy Spider*, with appropriate actions – and obvious enjoyment.

The whole PEEP programme 'focuses on how to make the most of everyday life at home… It builds on what parents already do, recognising babies' and young children's extraordinary capacity to learn.'

It begins right at the beginning; new babies are invited to join a PEEP group through their health visitor. Home visits may be offered in some cases, but there is much to be gained from the weekly group sessions. These allow discussion of a theme relating to children's development; there is time for carers to share experiences and support one another; and they may also borrow equipment for use at home.

Research has shown that the 0 to 4 year-olds benefit enormously from PEEP, and a study is currently under way into how the early education partnership also builds the self-confidence of the carers.

The Sleeper Path Project – a contribution from JRHT (November 2004)

Since before the summer holidays a group of young people from New Earswick/Huntington/Haxby have been working together to renovate the garden at the back of the Sleeper Path Project building (at the end of Station

Avenue). They are developing the garden into a space which can be used for young people's activities, events and workshops. The group have worked alongside City of York Council Youth Workers and are making good progress with the garden. Here is what one young girl (aged 14) had to say about it:

'We have been working on the garden since June, to provide a place for young people in the village to chill out, do activities, have barbecues etc. The work has included getting rid of weeds (which were about six foot high before we began work), digging, levelling the soil, laying a membrane, spreading gravel over the ground and laying pavement. We will begin planting plants and shrubs in the spring, when we hope the garden will be ready for other young people to use.

The gardening project was fun, and kept us out of trouble over the summer holiday. It gave us something to do. We also attended a Drop-in session over the holidays, every Tuesday, where we were able to play games, listen to music and chill out. We got ideas together about how to raise money for the Sleeper Path Project and took part in a visit to City

Screen cinema, where we watched a film, used the computers and learned how to use a video camera.'

During spring 2005 the gardening project will continue, when we will be able to do some planting. We will then be holding an open day, when the garden will be open for residents to come and see the transformation.

Look out for details in the Bulletin next spring!

Thanks again to all the young people who took part, for all their time, hard work and dedication. You are the ones who made this possible!

HOTEY – a contribution from JRHT (February 2005)

The Helping Others To Enjoy Yourself project has been developed with young people and is based around young people helping in the community. In return for helping they will 'earn' points which they will be able to exchange for rewards.

Each activity will be overseen by a designated responsible adult, and have a pre-determined point value which, once the activity is completed will be 'banked' for future use to go on a trip or participate in an activity.

Examples of the activities we are intending to include are gardening, painting, leaflet production and delivery. The activities available will increase as the project develops.

Young people will register on the scheme and get a membership card and book to record their points. The rewards will consist of organised trips and activities arranged by JRHT and the Youth Service, and run by volunteers, youth workers, police, estate caretakers etc.

If you are a young person who would like to join the scheme, an adult who would like to help supervise some of the activities or if you have an idea for an activity which could be part of the scheme, please ring Julie Boyes.

HOTEY Garden Project – a contribution from JRHT (October 2005)

This summer has seen our young HOTEY volunteers involved in some gardening. (HOTEY stands for Helping Others To Enjoy Yourself.) The projects took place in the gardens of local residents who are disabled, elderly or frail, and unable to do their gardening themselves. The young people's team worked tirelessly to weed and tidy flower beds and paths, making good use of the Trust's garden refuse recycling at Sleeper Path by disposing of all the unwanted waste.

For example, the team visited Mrs McGill of Station Avenue, who commented, "It's just marvellous, the children and adult supervisors were wonderful and worked ever so well. It makes things easier for me, and I'd like to thank the group for all their hard work as it has greatly enhanced the appearance of my already wonderful garden, thanks again."

The gardening scheme runs throughout the summer and rewards the young people for contributing to their community with points which are then cashed in for prizes. The project is open for any young people in the village. For further information please contact Julie Boyes.

Swimming Club Open Day – by the Club Secretary (November 2006)

On Saturday 30 September, New Earswick Swimming Club held an Open Day at the pool to promote the Club.

Taster swimming lessons were held for children, along with a recreational session for families. The Club held a tombola, raffle, guess the name of the gorilla and many other activities, raising £300 towards the Club's funds, which will go towards the funding of new equipment for the Club.

The Club is currently accepting membership applications for new members. Anyone interested should contact the Secretary. The Management Committee of the Club would like to say a big thank you to everyone who helped make the day a success.

New Earswick All Blacks – from the New Earswick Amateur Rugby League FC (May 2006)

New Earswick All Blacks ARLFC runs from New Earswick Sports and Social Club on White Rose Avenue. With approximately 200 players, boys and girls from 6 years old to open age, it is fair to say that New Earswick All

Blacks have one of the most thriving Rugby League sections in Yorkshire.

For twenty years the club has provided the York community with the opportunity to participate in the sport of Rugby League. The All Blacks are a volunteer organisation with over 15 qualified coaches. Each team

New Earswick All Blacks in action.

has at least one First Aid badge-holder, an assistant coach, and a secretary who, together with its members and loyal, dedicated parents and players, contribute to ensure that its traditions and camaraderie are carried forward for future generations. Because of this loyal support, our club is going from strength to strength, and has gained the Sport England Clubmark, a nationally recognised award for our dedication to the safety, protection and coaching of our players.

Many of our players have an extremely bright future in Rugby League; we have had several representing

England, many of our older junior teams have already been signed up on scholarships to professional clubs, and numerous players represent our county in the Yorkshire Service Area.

We welcome this opportunity to share our successes with the local community by way of the *Bulletin* every month, and hope that you, the readers, will give us your support over the seasons.

Our under 8s team has players ranging from 6 to 8 years old; their coach is former Wakefield, Sheffield and York player Chris Judge, who also plays for our flourishing Open Age team. Their season restarted on 12 March and already they have shown they are a team to look out for in the next decade.

Our outstanding under 9s team remained undefeated from September to December and continued this success at the start of the second half of the season on 12 March. New players are now being recruited for this team as well as for our under 10s team which is in the top division, playing some of the most successful teams in Yorkshire.

The young players in the under 11s team, now in the second half of their season, are gearing themselves up for next season when they hope to be as successful as our current under 12s team, coached by Simon Malarkey, who is currently in the semi-finals of the Challenge Cup. This is the youngest of the competitive teams for which league tables and cup clashes emerge, and they are doing magnificently, lying second in the league with two games in hand. Their trial for the Service Area was held on 30 March at Joseph Rowntree School.

Our under 13s team is coached by former York player, Phil Poole. They are another of our successes, with players representing Yorkshire, and the team is currently taking part in the Yorkshire League's Continuation Cup together with our thriving under 14s team. Some of these players are on scholarships with York City Knights, and we wish them every success.

Our under 15s team is coached by former York player, Rich Hayes, and is full of exceptional players. Three have signed up for York City Knights, two have signed for Hull and one has not only signed for Hull K R but has also been picked for England Under 15s. Our under 15s are in the semi-finals of the Continuation Cup and are in joint 4th place in the whole league. Their trial for the Service Area was held on Tuesday 28 March at Joseph Rowntree School. Some of these players have even been picked to represent their county in Rugby Union.

The Under 15s girls' team is also hugely successful; they are coached by former Great Britain player Julie Cole. This is the girls' first season at competitive level and one of them has been picked to represent Yorkshire.

Hayley Fairclough, picked for Yorkshire.

New Earswick All Blacks Youth team, the Under 16s, coached by former Castleford and York coach and player Stuart Hatan, has had an excellent season. Five or six of these players attend the same school and reached the Powergen School Cup final – some were also asked to play Rugby Union and managed to reach the semi-finals in this game as well. Many of these players have also been signed up to play for professional clubs.

Our Open Age team has been going from strength to strength over the last few seasons, under the excellent coaching skills of Simon Baines and ex-York player Alan Pallister. Last season they were promoted to Pennine League Division One and through their dedication are now in 2nd place in this league, hoping for promotion into the Premier Division.

Junior Angling Club – by Michael Longhurst (August 2006)

Regular readers may remember an advert placed in the *New Earswick Bulletin* a couple of years ago asking any young people interested in taking up fishing to contact us. The resulting interest led to our first junior coaching scheme being run in the middle of 2004 with 14 young people taking part.

Since then over forty young people have attended the three coaching courses that we have run. These courses are run over several weeks and provide a basic introduction to angling. The courses are led by a licensed coach who has completed the Level 2 Certificate in Coaching Angling, a national qualification recognised by Sport England, along with many voluntary helpers who assist the young people during coaching sessions. One of the factors that has made the course so successful is the support provided by these volunteers. Most have been involved with the scheme from the start and are an invaluable asset.

Another aspect to the Coaching Scheme is the holding of regular 'taster sessions' at Nature Reserve Open Days. (The next one will be on 19 August 2006.) These are twenty-minute sessions where anyone can turn up and fish. Helpers are on hand to assist and anyone wishing to take up the sport can talk to our coaches. This is also an ideal way of recruiting young people for the Junior Coaching Scheme as it gives everyone a chance to get to

know each other.

Our Junior Angling Club continues to grow and currently has seventeen members all of whom have successfully completed the coaching course. A further article detailing their activities will be appearing in the *New Earswick Bulletin* later this year.

We have just completed the training of a second coach to help increase the number of people we can support and, although all tackle and bait is provided during the coaching course, we are always looking for old tackle for our members to use. To donate items please contact Vic Atkins or George Leaf.

Living Longer – But Where? (November 2005)

Old People: report of a survey committee on the problems of ageing and the care of old people is the title of the Nuffield report published in 1947. The survey committee had worked on it for two years, chaired by Seebohm Rowntree. Once the report was completed, he wasted no time in acting on its recommendations; and where better to start than right here in New Earswick?

By 1947 a number of residents, who had moved to the village in its early years, were now unable to look after themselves. Many of them had had to move to care homes in Scarborough or Whitby, far from family and friends.

One who refused to move was an old lady who lived, alone and in need of care, in one of the four-bedroom houses in Western Terrace. In those days the housing manager used to collect the rent in person, and she came to know tenants so well that she was also able to tackle their welfare needs. (Of course, the village was much smaller then than it is now.) Eventually she reached a compromise with the old lady who, very naturally, wanted to stay where she was. She was persuaded to take a holiday, at the expense of the Trust, while 'her' house was converted into a mini-care home for four residents in need of care. Furniture and equipment were provided by the Trust for the dining and sitting rooms. Upstairs, each bedroom became a bed-sitter furnished by its occupant, and the old lady was able to stay in her favourite room. All four residents were looked after by a live-in warden and a helper from the village.

Another need highlighted in the Nuffield report was for small houses near the shops and other amenities. Here the elderly could lead independent lives, but help would be within call: what we now call sheltered housing. After considerable research and consultation, an innovative design was produced by the architect: it featured a bedroom and living room which could be quite separate, or used as one large room. Twelve cottages were built in a semi-circle in Lime Tree Avenue: eleven for elderly people and one for a retired nurse, who lived there rent-free in return for being on hand in case of need.

Then the old farmhouse we know as The Garth became vacant. By 1951 it had been converted into sheltered accommodation for eight or nine residents and two staff.

The Trust had also built 14 bungalows for elderly people; in 1954, the date of its 50th anniversary, another 10 were under construction. (For more about the Trust's first half century, read *One Man's Vision* by Lewis Waddilove, available from New Earswick library.)

Re-building Red Lodge was the next stage in the Trust's ongoing experiment. Originally a hostel for single women, it was demolished in 1976 and replaced by a block of self-contained flats, with a large dining/common room on the first floor. Later, an extension was added to the rear, providing apartments for 35 more able people. The front is reserved for 42 residential care occupants, some with a high level of dependency.

The continuing care retirement communities which had been established in the United States and in Germany now attracted the attention of the Trust. They provide for independence, with care available as and when required, at one location. The obvious advantages of this led the Trust to plan its own project partly on the Old School Playing Field. Although the application for planning permission was turned down by the Secretary of State, it was agreed that it was an important innovation and that the Trust was well-placed to establish a pilot scheme.

The pilot scheme, re-named Hartrigg Oaks, was eventually built on the other side of Haxby Road and opened in April 1998. Since then the Housing Trust has pursued its policy of developing different types of continuing care retirement communities. Bedford Court in Leeds, 'a test bed for a new flexible skill mix,' opened in July 2004.

On the research side, the Joseph Rowntree Foundation recently published a discussion paper, *Care for the Elderly*. In response, the policy manager for Help the Aged, said '... with a one in five chance of ending up in care, we must all plan ahead for the possibility of one day needing long term care.'

A Fifth Birthday   (April 2003)

Five years ago, on 1st and 2nd April 1998, the first residents moved into Hartrigg Oaks.   There were four of them and they came from Devon, Edinburgh and Shropshire.

It was still virtually a building site then: one third of the bungalows were completed, the Oaks Centre was not fully open, and the grounds were mostly mud. Those of us who moved in at the beginning have watched with great interest as work proceeded – and not just building work.

There were some teething problems to begin with, particularly about how the 'care package' was working out. But we now have two first-rate teams of carers, the 'lavender lassies' (because of the colour they wear) for the bungalow residents and a separate team for the care home.   The latter are also 'colour-coded': general assistants wear green and then there are various shades of blue, navy being for the senior nursing staff. Heard but not seen are the daily check-up telephone calls to those residents who have requested them. And of course, in common with Lifeline residents who live in other parts of New Earswick, we are all connected to an emergency call system.

After five years we can see for ourselves the advantages of having a care home on site. People needing to convalesce after a spell in hospital can have a room in The Oaks. On a very few occasions, room has had to be found elsewhere, on a temporary basis. The decision about whether a permanent move to The Oaks is necessary is taken over a period of several months. Indeed, it has been possible for some stroke sufferers to move back to their bungalows.

It is good to see how people with varying difficulties have been able to join in the many activities organised by residents. An obvious example is the Art Group, some of whose members turn up in wheelchairs, electric buggies, or using zimmer frames and walking sticks. Increasing numbers of visitors come to the art show held each autumn.

It's an odd quirk of human nature that no sooner have we found somewhere to live where almost everything is on tap, than we want to get away for the day! Those new to this part of the country particularly want to see as much of it as possible. So another residents' group, one which requires much detailed preparation, was established – Discovering Yorkshire. This, like concert and theatre outings and weekly shopping trips, is organised entirely by residents. All together there are over thirty special interest groups.

One of the most noticeable features of the last five years has been the greening of the grounds. First the grass was laid down, and what excitement that created!   Then came the trees and shrubs, carefully chosen to give year-round colour. Last but by no means least came residents' own gardens, reflecting individual taste. Some prefer a 'minimalist' garden, consisting simply of pebbles and a water feature; others go for colour and there are a few mini-greenhouses, where residents grow their own tomatoes.   I am reminded of Kipling's lines: 'And some can pot begonias and some can

Statue of the Hart outside the Oaks Centre.

bud a rose, And some are hardly fit to trust with anything that grows'!   I come into the latter category myself, but I blame the poor soil. This has been overcome in many gardens with compost from the Joseph Rowntree Housing Trust, and in some cases by the purchase of good-quality topsoil.

So far I have only written about the human occupation of Hartrigg Oaks, but the presence of birds gives great pleasure.   Residents on the south side enjoy the many smaller birds which can escape at the slightest alarm to the shelter of the nearby trees.   On the west, there is the beck with its convoys of ducks and the occasional sight of kingfishers.   The long-established hedge bordering Park Avenue is home to other species, particularly the songbirds.   In the centre of Hartrigg Oaks on the large grassed areas, we see wagtails, blackbirds, magpies and others, either pecking at the ground or visiting the bird tables which residents have set up in their gardens.

New Earswick is known as a garden village and it is hoped that Hartrigg Oaks will continue to become an integral part of both the garden and the village.

CHAPTER SEVEN

Some Disappointments

The following statement by Lewis Waddilove may be found in his book *One Man's Vision*, (1954) an account of the first 50 years of the village. He served as Executive Officer of the Trust.

'The battle for better housing and wider educational opportunity has been won, although the field is not yet fully occupied. But our society has yet to solve the problem of the social waste, and the loss of human happiness from generation to generation, in families apparently unable to profit from the opportunities open to them.'

Farewell to the Skateboard Ramp – by Peter Spavin, NERF Secretary (August 2001)

In the summer of 1999, the City of York Council provided a new resource for the young people of New Earswick and the surrounding area – a new, expensive and purpose-built skateboard ramp on the Playing Field. It proved to be immensely popular and wheeled enthusiasts converged on it from far and near, on roller skates, roller blades, skateboards and BMX bikes. Beginners tackled it, advanced users displayed their skills – and often looked after and helped the less able; even adults were observed surreptitiously having a go when few people were around.

There were complaints however; several people complained that the noise of wheels drummed like thunder throughout the summer evenings and disturbed their 'quiet enjoyment' of their homes - but after all, this was the playing field and where better to put it? One resident complained that as the ends of the ramp were raised it would be possible to see into her garden and even in through her windows. As a member of the Village Forum I duly went to see – and confirmed that it would indeed be possible to observe the activity in the nearest houses; if the curtains were open, the lights on and if the skater had had the foresight to bring a pair of binoculars.

There was a litter problem, true, but the Joseph Rowntree Housing Trust undertook to clear the area daily. It did not always seem that this was being done satisfactorily, but the situation did improve somewhat.

There were, of course, the pessimists. 'It's pointless spending this sort of money on the young people – they'll only destroy it, like they do anything worthwhile.' It soon began to seem as if they had a point. The pristine appearance of the new structure didn't last twenty-four hours, and within a week it had already accumulated sufficient graffiti to start to qualify as an eyesore. Personally, I have no objection to graffiti, as long as it's good – but the 'tags' of the local notorious, and gratuitous obscenity, don't qualify. Shortly thereafter, a hole was excavated in the upper decking, and a sort of stinking 'pack-rats nest' established in the bowels of the thing – old carpets, litter, empty drinks cans and worse. The City Council made several attempts to seal this off – but the boarding was ripped away every time and finally, the decking had to be clad with sheet metal.

Meanwhile, a sustained assault was made on the surrounding safety barrier. Inch thick planks were smashed to pieces and dragged off the supporting uprights – apparently, most of the time, in total silence; as few people own to having heard anything. Several attempts were made to set the thing ablaze – always with very limited success; and several areas of the skating surface were stove in.

So, who was responsible for all this vandalism? Young people – *bored* young people, who had neither the art nor the wit to appreciate that this had been provided to help with that condition and to use it properly. Young people whose answer to boredom is to get drunk and destroy or damage something (phone boxes, bus-shelters etc.) but who would be the first to complain if it were something of theirs. All the people who heard the destruction and thought, 'None of my business – let someone else deal with it'. The Police – who, when they were called, repeatedly took several HOURS to respond.

Certainly, not the young people who use it. Up until yesterday, people were still using it. Despite the holes in the surface, despite the lack of safety railings; despite even the City Council's barriers, intended to keep them off it. I saw a young man pick himself up, bleeding profusely after taking a tumble. 'Never mind,' he remarked, 'it's only a flesh wound.' And he carried on. Every day this summer, in fair weather or even foul, there have been enthusiastic users trundling back and forth delighting themselves and passers-by with their acrobatics. These people are losers in this.

But so are we all. As I write this, the skateboard ramp is being demolished and removed. It has been too badly damaged to be worth repairing. The vandals have won yet again.

Playground Provision – an account by Peter Spavin, NERF Secretary, of an Open Meeting of the Residents' Forum (September 2001)

Once again this was a lively and well-attended event. The members of the Executive attempted to deal with a number of issues raised by concerned residents. We were a little hampered by the fact that we received last minute apologies from P.C. Dave Ward, our new Community Policeman. Although it was his rest day he had assured us that he would attend, and consequently many of the matters that had been brought to the meeting concerned policing and problems that villagers thought required his attention.

Concern was expressed about the nocturnal activities in the bushes at the back of Woodland Place – apparently there are all sorts of goings on. There were complaints of drunken youths, drugs, noise, rubbish (including items of furniture) and on at least one occasion someone running wild with an air rifle. Apparently, representations to the police had, overall, produced a less than acceptable response and our Community Policeman had been very little help.

Residents were also concerned about the Trust's policy in the area, which had allowed the section of land there and adjacent to the children's play area to degenerate into a wilderness – apparently to create a 'wild-life habitat'. The comment was that it seemed to be attracting totally the wrong type of 'wild-life'. There was no representative of the Trust present to comment on the matter, but the overwhelming consensus of the meeting was that this area should be cleared and once more brought within the properly cultivated areas of the village.

One of the village residents, who works in close contact with many of the village teenagers, identified the main problem as being boredom and felt that perhaps our approach to their problems was wrong; that maybe we were presenting the young people with 'so-called' answers designed by us, the older generation, rather than involving them in the decision-making structure and allowing them to devise their own solutions and make them work. It was pointed out that the young people were actively involved in the planning and construction of the Youth Shelter, in the activities and running of the Sleeper Path Project and had asked for the provision of the Skateboard Ramp, now sadly destroyed by others. There is a continual effort to get young people involved in planning for their own activities, and to engage them with the community as a whole. There is, however, a 'hard core' of village youths who refuse to become involved and who take a negative approach to everything; whose attitude, unfortunately, frequently seems to be condoned and their anti-social activities even encouraged by their parents.

Several of the residents present asked that we revert to the matter of the 'Woodlands' play park. They felt, as mothers or grandmothers with toddlers to entertain, that the provision of play facilities in the village was totally inadequate. This particular play area was isolated, bordering an area that was now overgrown and unsavoury, and was far too near to the river. It was now only used during the day by older children on the way to and from the Joseph Rowntree School or on their lunch-break; and in the evening by the 'mob'. It was totally failing to serve its purpose as a play area for toddlers, as none of those present felt that they would ever feel safe or comfortable taking their children there – and, in fact, none of them used it. Some went to Rowntrees Park or the Homestead – but others could not travel or did not have transport, and all would be much happier if there were better resources locally.

It was agreed that, ideally, this play area should be closed and the equipment relocated in a more suitable area. There were two suggestions: firstly, the grassed area on Alder Way, opposite Aucuba Close (subject to the problem of dog fouling being resolved), and secondly, in Ivy Place. The advantage of both of these areas was that they were overlooked from all sides and there were no current problems, even though one already has some play equipment on it. It was also hoped that some more adventurous equipment could be provided – the climbing frame has been greatly missed. There was also criticism of the 'wood chippings surface' of the play area on the playing field behind the Folk Hall. Apparently it has been discovered, from time to time, to conceal used syringes and broken glass. It was agreed that we should press for rubberised surfaces on all toddlers' playing areas to prevent this. We appointed a sub-committee from those attending this meeting to contact the relevant officers of the Trust, progress these matters and report back to the next Open Meeting.

Residents in the Alder Way have organised a petition to request that dogs be banned from the play space on Alder Way, opposite Aucuba Close. This follows repeated instances of dog fouling in a children's play area. All present agreed that the fencing around this area should be completed – there is presently open access at the Garth Way end of the grassed area – and that notices should be posted.

Somewhere to Hang Out (May 2006)

'Young people resent being seen as a problem and often consider themselves as the victims. They complain about a lack of facilities and often wish to be involved in finding solutions to the problems.' This statement comes from the *Good Practice Guide to Youth Shelters and Sporting*

Facilities, a document commissioned by the Thames Valley Police from the University of the West of England in Bristol. It says that young people want somewhere to

go that is safe, where they won't get hassled: a place of their own away from adults, and that they should be consulted as how this would best be provided.

Working with the local school would seem a logical way to do this, and the authors suggest using curriculum-based activities, such as running a design competition for a youth shelter. Scale drawings of the winning ideas could be produced in the technical drawing class. Other suggestions are for the geography students to survey possible sites, the maths students to evaluate data, and so on.

They also emphasise the benefit of involving the young people in fund-raising. Besides giving practice in writing to possible sponsors, it gives them a sense of ownership. This feeling of responsibility can be handed on to the future groups of teenagers, by re-painting the shelter and by raising more money for maintenance or improvements.

In Witney, the residents' association, the housing association and the police set up a working party together with the youth worker. The latter's task was to discuss the options with the young people. He met them outside the shops, to discuss what they wanted and to study the catalogues. The style, colour and location of the shelter were their choice. A snag arose when the local council withheld planning permission because the seat was to be bright mauve! In the end all parties settled for green. The result was a shelter that is well-used, 'although there are always some who favour sitting on the stairs that lead to the flats above the shops.'

Many of the designs for shelters shown in the catalogues are more suited to a site on the moon than a conservation area like New Earswick. A lot of them are brightly coloured tubular constructions, open on all sides with only the roof as a protection against the weather. So partial screening is recommended. The *Good Practice Guide* advises that they should not be too enclosed because people can feel trapped in them and no one can see inside.

When New Earswick's youth shelter was built, the Joseph Rowntree Housing Trust worked on the proposal with the police, youth workers and about 15 young people. These were contacted through the youth groups existing at the time (1999). Plans were on display at the Folk Hall, and on seeing these, residents recommended moving the shelter from the north west corner of the Rec. to its present position. The cost of about £10,000 was met by the Safer Partnership and the York Challenge Fund (both City of York Council); this included a contribution of £2,500 from New Earswick Parish Council.

Research initiated by Haxby Town Council for their *2020 Vision a plan for the future of Haxby* highlighted the need for a safe and attractive environment. There were four questionnaires altogether, two of them designed for the younger generation, so that even the 7 to 11 year-olds had their say. The results showed that the places they disliked most were the alleyway from South Lane through to Ryedale Court and the public toilets in the arcade. They liked the Ethel Ward playing field and much of their spare time was spent at home or at a friend's house. As you would expect, the 12 to 17 year-olds were ready to spread their wings, wanting to 'socialise with their friends in a safe and congenial location' on an informal and irregular basis. They fancied having a place where anything from a cup of coffee to a hot meal was available, where there was access to computers, where they could make live music, play recorded music, dance, or watch special events on a large screen TV – quite a wish list!

This bears out the point made in the introduction to the *Good Practice Guide*: 'Youth shelters are not the whole solution ... Failure to invest in facilities that young people want is a false economy.'

Getting the Decorators In – by Carole Farrar, Headteacher of New Earswick Primary School (November 2004)

In June, New Earswick Primary School applied for a York Community Pride Grant to improve the appearance of the Youth Shelter, which stands adjacent to the school on the village green. The school was notified they would receive a grant in early September; then it was all systems go to complete the project.

Since it was built around five years ago, the shelter has been a target for vandalism, graffiti and anti-social behaviour. The school has long been concerned that children were witnessing the results of such behaviour on their daily journey to school and wanted to try to do something to improve the situation.

The idea of painting a mural on the inside of the shelter proved popular with the children, who were excited by the opportunity to work with professional mural artist Griselda Goldsbrough. The children realised they would have to come up with something that would appeal to older teenagers – whilst fluffy bunnies and nursery rhyme scenes might be attractive to them, they realised teenagers might feel differently! The school council took the lead at the design stage – getting ideas from their classmates and liaising with the artist.

The project took some organising as it involved around 240 children! The school was grateful for the volunteer help it received with the project, and also for the support of the Joseph Rowntree Housing Trust in ensuring the shelter area was clean and safe for the children to work in. Many older youths commented how much they liked what the children were doing and were impressed by the artistic talent on display!

We really hoped that the children's work would get the respect it deserves, but unfortunately, a few young people have felt the need to spoil the mural already. Whilst this is disappointing, the experience of taking part in producing a work of art will stay with our pupils forever. Also, the project has helped prompt some valuable debates and learning about anti-social behaviour, which we hope will help shape our pupils' development as caring and responsible citizens of the future.

How Long Does it Take? – by the Editorial Sub-Group (February 2004)

In last month's edition we asked the question, 'How long does it take before an "Acceptable Behaviour

Commitment" contract is enforced?' and the Housing Services Manager has promised us a full response for our March edition. We look forward to this. In the mean time, however, another month has passed during which our lives have been plagued by anti-social behaviour.

On page 9 of this issue the Parish Council gives details of the cost of repairing bus shelters damaged by vandalism. It comes to £2,061 so far, although these figures do not include the damage done to the bus shelter opposite the Folk Hall on Saturday 3 January. We are warned that this expenditure may have a direct impact on the size of our forthcoming Council Tax contributions.

On page 12 there is some good advice from PC Paul Beckwith on how to avoid having your car subjected to autocrime. This is especially welcome, as he says that during the last twelve months almost £15,000 worth of property was stolen from unattended vehicles in New Earswick.

But the damage is not confined to our bus shelters and our cars. On the evening of Monday 5 January, a number of youths caused so much nuisance at the New Earswick Library that the Librarian closed early and phoned for the Mayfair Security rangers to help her. They were unable to attend immediately, so she locked up and left the premises, after which the youths broke in and were able to avoid triggering the alarm system. The Head Librarian has now arranged for a security guard to be on duty at the Library on Monday evenings to help the Library staff maintain order. But this did not prevent the breaking of yet another Library window on Tuesday 13 January. We understand that the cost of damage to the Library during the last twelve months is approaching

£2,000. What kind of impact will that have on our Council Tax demands?

In a recent report to Communities that Care, the Community Services Manager wrote: 'At New Earswick Library... the group for young men who have been involved in anti-social behaviour has been very successful...'

We find this difficult to understand. On page 13 of this issue you will see details of The Venue, one of the Library's positive initiatives for young people. This is a particularly valuable example of the benefits which our community derives from its Library, and one which is now threatened by the violent behaviour of a small group of young thugs.

The list goes on. On the weekend of 3 January a window was broken at the Friends Meeting House. During the early evening of Saturday 10 January, a group of youths and young women took a fire extinguisher from the Folk Hall, and began spraying its contents over traffic in the road outside. Only the prompt action of an off-duty policeman who happened to be passing prevented what could otherwise have become a dangerous situation. On Monday 12 January yet one more of the Folk Hall windows was broken.

We are fortunate to live in a community which has the capacity to apply sanctions to those who persist in anti-social behaviour. What worries us is that apparently the will to apply those sanctions is lacking.

On Tuesday 3 February there will be an Open Meeting of the New Earswick Residents' Forum (7.30 p.m. at the Folk Hall). The main item on the agenda is Security in New Earswick. If you feel, as we do, that this issue needs some open discussion, do try and make time to attend.

CHAPTER EIGHT

Community Spirit

Bridging the Generation Gap at Red Lodge – by Julie Boyes of JRHT (April 2003)

This month saw two local young people join five older residents at Red Lodge to produce an inter-generational piece of mosaic work. Many thanks to Pam Smith who organised the Red Lodge side of things and proved a fantastic support on the day. The afternoon was brilliant with the group deciding together on tropical animals. The older residents were very welcoming and encouraging with our young people, making it a fun relaxed atmosphere. The young people really enjoyed chatting away with the older residents. The group spoke about their planned artwork, their skills (all said they weren't very good at art, younger and older), their life in New Earswick, and making curd tarts. The young people gave out cream cakes at the break.

The finished piece is worthy of the Tate. Two snakes interweave between flowers, insects and trees. The project was so successful it ran over by an hour. Because the young people involved were also HOTEY members, it was decided they should receive points for being such impressive ambassadors. An excellent start to some possible future inter-generational work.

If you would like to get involved in this or other youth projects please contact Julie Boyes.

New Earswick Community Philosophy Project – by Helen Mackenzie (October 2006)

What a fantastic day for our first intergenerational trip outside New Earswick this year. The sun was shining and everyone arrived on time for our day out. The residents at Red Lodge and some of the younger people had already met on a few occasions, and the venue for the joint excursion was discussed between us all and decided earlier on in the summer. The young people had visited the residents at Red Lodge and discussed the ideal venue for the trip, taking into consideration the needs of all the participants. This was followed on a separate occasion by a friendly bowls match in order to get to know some of the older people better before the big day. Arnold gave them some great bowling tips and they did well.

There were 25 of us in total, 9 residents from Red Lodge with Pam Smith and Brenda Parnaby, 9 young people from the village and 2 volunteers. We watched *Sharks* (a three-dimensional film) together. Everyone really enjoyed it and Arnold, who is partially sighted, was also able to enjoy the experience too. Many people said, 'It really felt as if the fish were coming out of the screen towards us.' Thanks go to everyone who took part in the event.

Conversation is the Key (October 2006)

'Conversation' says my book of *Etiquette for Ladies and Gentlemen*, 'is a pleasing and instructive method of spending an evening after the fatigues of business, and one often resorted to by all classes.' This little gem from Victorian times came to mind when I was told of a new scheme to develop the conversational skills of Sixth Formers: in this case, those attending the Joseph Rowntree School, in collaboration with some of its neighbours opposite at Hartrigg Oaks.

A 'pleasing and instructive' conversation arises from a common interest, preferably with different views on that topic. For example, looking at art exhibitions produces a variety of opinions about the same picture – its subject, its medium and the skill of the artist. Last year students from the Joseph Rowntree School were invited to the annual art exhibition organised by the Hartrigg Oaks Art Group and the comments printed in the *Hartrigg Oaks News* are an indication of the conversations it stimulated. In May of this year, about ten members of the art group visited the much bigger final show of A level art and design at the school. Set up in about six different rooms, it included an impressive variety of work, such as painting on silk, papier maché and pottery: plenty to talk about there!

Christmas events also produced contacts between Hartrigg Oaks and the younger generation. Advent was celebrated by the German Group and guests from the school; the singing of German carols was followed by a delicious selection of food featuring some traditional German baking. As for the conversation, they did their best to stick to talking German to both the 'oldies' from Hartrigg Oaks and to each other.

A couple of days later, the Cercle Français ran a similar event for students studying French, and their report concludes: 'It was a particular delight to meet our younger neighbours with a shared interest.'

The initiative for these occasions came from the school staff, who put forward no fewer than nine ways in which collaboration could be developed. In addition to the group activities described above, there were proposals for individual contacts. Mock interviews for students preparing for university or employment was one and mentoring another.

Research on mentoring, commissioned by the Joseph Rowntree Foundation a few years ago, has produced some interesting findings. Mentoring is a befriending scheme in which young people can share similar backgrounds and experiences with an adult who will respect their confidentiality. It is distinguished from other forms of help by its friendly nature and 'the ability to have a laugh'. It is interesting to note that the four-page summary of the research emphasises the advantage of sharing a laugh in this specialised relationship.

Matching a vulnerable young person with a suitable mentor requires considerable skill and Percy Roberts, a school governor, has been handling this. Percy has lived in New Earswick for many years and has had a long career in adult education; also very important (in my view!) is his experience as the grandfather of six, whose ages range from 15 to 21 years.

There has been much discussion recently about the value of intergenerational work in overcoming misunderstandings in the community. Many readers will recall, as a grandparent or a grandchild, how much easier it was to talk to someone of the next generation but one. Skipping a generation can be an effective solution to what the *Mature Times* describes as 'many of society's most deeply rooted problems.' It goes on to say: 'The grandparent generation (and in this you can include great aunts and uncles) has always played a huge and invariably positive part in youngsters' lives and provided additional role models.' Conversation is surely a key factor in this approach.

TimeChange (January 2007)

All the world certainly was a stage for this unusual piece of theatre performed by two New Earswick generations: the older actors from Hartrigg Oaks and the drama students from the Joseph Rowntree School. They were brought together by Riding Lights, a theatre company founded in York about thirty years ago. Its aim is to stage high quality productions reaching a broad audience. TimeChange was a unique theatrical story-exchange between generations, hence its title.

For the first time in this country, live acting and digital storytelling (introduced by Digistories) were combined to

share memories. Many of these were of children's games, one example being cowboys and Indians. The male members of the cast (both young and old), equipped with cowboy hats and guns, staged a lively fight. They fell to the floor when shot, rolling about in realistic agony. The female actors then made an entrance, wearing fetching feather headdresses, and comforted the wounded. Days at school produced stories from both generations, not a few about school dinners. One story was about the pupils banging on the dinner tables in protest against something long forgotten. What stuck in the storyteller's mind was the way the headmistress (Dame Dorothy by name) dealt with the incident, reminding the pupils to show respect to others.

Work experience is an aspect of modern day schooling completely new to the older generation.   It was amusingly illustrated by one of the young actors acting the roles of himself and his four co-workers. This little scene helped the audience to understand, and to remember, what it must have been like.

The use of old photographs, projected onto a large screen was effective in recreating the days of long ago. There was a soundtrack some of the of the storytellers' voices, and present day portraits – some 70 years later in one case – were also featured. An impressive piece of technical wizardry involved a sequence of shots of a mechanical digger tilted at ever increasing angles, giving the illusion that it was careering downhill. (This was part of a story about digging a trench across a steep slope to in order to ensure that the soak-away no longer carried unpleasant smells downhill to the neighbouring property.)

Eleven weeks of hard work went into this production. Following an introductory social meeting, the two groups and their tutors worked separately for the first seven weeks, assembling memories and photographs from which Paul Birch, the Riding Lights education officer, composed a structured result – reduced from a total of 31,000 words! Attention was paid to continuity, so that one reminiscence flowed into another, occasionally taking on a conversational format.

The familiar broadcast statements by Chamberlain and Churchill served to introduce war-time memories. Even the destruction of New York's twin towers by terrorists brought personal recollections from both generations. In describing where they were at the time and how the news affected them, the shock felt by both actors came over with sincerity.

The last four weeks really tested the commitment of the whole cast. Rehearsals were lengthy; slick scene-shifting of tables and chairs had to be perfected and special effects tried out. One of these represented a huge sentry challenging a little boy in the total blackout of war time. To make the sentry more terrifying, one actor cloaked in black, was carried on the shoulders of another; he pointed a (dummy) rifle down at the cowering child, in the person of his older, grown-up self.

Finally, returning to the theme of 'all the world's a stage' from *As You Like It*, we heard the speech describing the seven stages of life. These were mimed by the Joseph Rowntree students. Their sense of fun shone out in the portrayal of 'the whining schoolboy ...creeping like snail unwillingly to school', but the 'last scene of all', the death scene, was done with convincing solemnity.

Thanks from the cast to Riding Lights, Digistories, and the teachers at the Joseph Rowntree School met with enthusiastic applause. The words 'Well done' could be heard over and over again as audience and actors intermingled, making their way home from the Friargate Theatre. A second performance took place at Hartrigg Oaks.

Open Day at the Folk Hall (October 2007)

The programme for this event promised 'lots of fun for all the family.' It continued: 'The Folk Hall are proud to play host to many local groups,' and asked us to 'take this opportunity to have a chat or indulge an interest' in their activities as displayed on the tables and stands around the main hall.

Dropping in for a couple of hours was time well spent, but where were the hoped-for crowds? Apart from a notice in the *New Earswick Bulletin*, where was the other advance publicity? Where were the posters around the village and in shop windows? Where was the banner on the front of the Folk Hall? Why was the showcase on the side of the swimming pool still advertising a past event? Local groups had put in a lot of work on the preparation of their displays and they deserved a better turn-out.

Among these was the Allotment Society with a most attractive mini-harvest festival set out on their table. (We were assured that the tomatoes were delicious!) Besides some colourful examples of intricate beadwork, the Embroidery Guild had a stand on their table displaying 16 squares of Yorkshire's white rose, each one featuring a different kind of needlework beautifully executed. Knowing the value of advance publicity, the Musical Society seized the opportunity to advertise their new production of *Fiddler on the Roof,* opening in November.

Other organisations taking part were the Swimming Club, the Coronary Support Group, the North Yorkshire Women's Institute, the Family History Society and the Sensory Garden Project. The last-named held a supper dance in the evening.

Also represented was the New Earswick Parish Council; it rents an office in the Folk Hall, thus contributing funds to the New Earswick Community Association which runs the Hall. Among the people interested in the photographs and books which illustrated the responsibilities of the Parish Council were one fairly new resident and one who has lived here since 1923. The former moved here four years ago, is a member of the Musical Society and is most appreciative of the many trees and open spaces. (Incidentally, she also enjoys reading the *Bulletin.*) It was a joy to see the interest taken by the ninety-year old resident. He recalled the days before the main hall was built, when the site was occupied by two farm cottages. He looked at the minute books dating from the 1930s and '40s and was shown a photograph of the 1973 Parish Council, recognising familiar names and faces. Two of our parish councillors come from families who have lived locally for several generations and they were delighted to take part in one of those 'do you remember' conversations.

Besides the displays, there were demonstrations. Future

Prospects set up a laptop and printer in the Coffee Lounge to show what fun can be had with computer images. Members of the Aerobics Club went through a shortened version of their Tuesday evening programme giving us a taste of their weekly sessions. The line dancing demonstration included a number of dances starting with the simplest steps, and some of the audience joined in a later dance. Towards the end we watched a dance strongly influenced by Irish dancing. It was an intriguing mix.

Indeed, the Open Day itself was an intriguing mix and could well lead to future events of a similar nature – with comprehensive advertising, of course!

The Methodist Chapel's 80th Anniversary – by Elizabeth Jefferson (November 2007)

During the weekend of 21st to 23rd September, New Earswick Methodist Church celebrated its 80th Anniversary with a Festival of Flowers and a display of memorabilia. Whilst collecting items for the display, I learnt quite a lot about the history of Methodism and the church in New Earswick.

In August 1904, a meeting was held in the village, where a wish was expressed that a place be found where people could meet to worship. Two houses in Station Avenue were made available to the different religious groups and were called The New Earswick Assembly Rooms, the first Wesleyan Mission being held on 25th November 1904. When the Folk Hall was built in 1907, it became possible for a room there to be used for worship.

In 1911, the Methodists made a request to the Joseph Rowntree Trust that a piece of land be made available for the building of a Wesleyan Chapel. In 1914 the Village Trust offered a site for the erection of a Chapel within an agreed time at a stipulated cost, the building to be in harmony with the general architecture of the village, notably the school and the Folk Hall, the site being provided free of charge. The outbreak of war made it impossible to go on with this proposal and nothing definite was done until 1921. Eventually, an agreement was made that the chapel should cost no more than £3000 and the congregation undertook to raise £100 per year for the next five years. Bazaars, sewing meetings, concerts etc. were held on a regular basis. During this time, the congregation and Sunday School continued to meet at the Folk Hall, apart from August and September of 1914, when the Sunday School was closed due to Whooping Cough and Diphtheria epidemics in the village.

On 21st September 1927, the new Wesleyan Chapel was officially opened. The seating accommodation was for 130 and there was provision in the Sunday School for 150 scholars, the school room being partitioned off with the facility to open it up when more seating was required. The original plans for the opening service had been that everyone would assemble outside and sing the first hymn before the door was opened, but true to British weather, it rained and had to be abandoned. All the accommodation was utilized and many people had to stand at the back, the number present was almost 400!

In 1962 it was decided to build an extension, all the fund-raising started again with the new hall being opened in 1970.

During the years, there have been so many events, Jumble Sales, Christmas Fayres, Sunday School outings and Anniversaries, Beetle Drives, Concerts, Harvest Suppers, Eisteddfods, Youth Clubs, a lot of fun and laughter, tears and sadness, a lot of hard work, weddings from friendships formed through Church. There has been fellowship, worship and service. And we wanted to celebrate it all.

Earlier this year, we found old programmes for Aladdin and Cinderella Pantomimes, performed by members of the Church in the late 1940's. They were held in the Folk Hall and written and directed by Elsie Chown. The cast included many people I knew from my childhood, notably Margaret Dufton who played the Principal Boy in both productions. I contacted other people I knew, and some of the children of those who had died with an amazing response. People had photographs, Birthday cards, Scripture Exam, Junior Missionary Association and Eisteddfod Certificates, Sunday School Prizes and many other things they had forgotten about. It stirred up all sorts of memories and endless hours of reminiscing.

For the anniversary, we wanted a celebration of all the last 80 years, so we presented what is going on in the Church today, we have a friendly, hard working, although small membership, a thriving Girls' Brigade, are involved with the Junior School assemblies and very much looking forward to the future.

The flowers over the weekend were organized by Pam Smith. On the Sunday, we celebrated Harvest Festival and our Anniversary Service at which the Bible lesson was read by Margaret Dufton who was five years old when she attended the opening service with her parents (and can remember where she sat).

We had a wonderful weekend, meeting up with old friends and re-telling stories. I have enjoyed every minute of collecting the items and am very grateful to everyone who lent me their memories.

Queen's Award (September 2005)

After 2 years of hard work, Heidi Rigby of 3rd York Girls' Brigade at New Earswick Methodist Church has gained the highest award in the Girls' Brigade. Everyone at the Company is extremely proud of her especially as she is the first to win the award in the Company's 34-year history.

To achieve the award she helped at the St Leonard's Hospice charity shop in Haxby, produced a project on her life in the Girls' Brigade, undertook two initiative tests set by the District Commissioner, sat a written paper on the monarchy and government and had final assessments on her knowledge of the national and international Girls' Brigade.

Heidi has been a member of the Company for 13 years, progressing through each of the sections from Explorers to Brigaders and has recently become a Warrant Officer. She is now our Explorer leader working with girls aged 5-8 years. She is also a Millennium Volunteer.

Extension to the Friends Meeting House
(October 2002)

Many readers will have noticed the extension to the Friends' Meeting House at the end of the Folk Hall car park. For local Quakers this has been the culmination of years of discussion. We had been 'bursting at the seams' for long enough.

First, we had to choose an architect; we started with seven possibilities, then we narrowed it down to three and finally to one. What made us choose that one? Two of the reasons were practical: one was that his scheme would meet our needs at least expense, and the other was that the building work could be phased in such a way that our Sunday morning Meetings for Worship and children's classes could continue without interruption. (The third reason appears at the end of this article.)

What we wanted was a well-lit, square extension, large enough to seat 80 people, on the south side of the

existing building. Our architect produced idea after idea – and left the choice to us. He himself favoured a pyramidal roof, in keeping with the main building, but with a lantern at the peak. Light flooding down from above would certainly have been attractive – and inspirational – but what of the practicalities and would it harmonise with the neighbouring buildings?

A small group of Quakers went to visit a church in Gildersome (St Peters) to have a look at their lantern roof. And, as is often the way, they came back with a quite different suggestion. They had particularly liked the calm and peaceful atmosphere of the church library area, featuring a line of windows high up along one wall – a sort of clerestory. This solved the problem of windows at the south side of our extension, looking out on to the doctors' surgery. A decision about the west and east elevations still had to be reached. Should we have floor to ceiling windows and glass doors, along one side? What about a pergola? What about security? What about the doors at the front?

Our patient architect drew sketch after sketch and we sat round watching, rather like children being amused by a grown-up. At last, before our very eyes, the way forward became clear. What we saw roughed out with a felt-tip pen that day has now become our new building.

Deciding how to alter the existing meeting house was comparatively simple: divide the large room into two by means of an acoustic folding screen, remove some of the internal walls to create a bigger circulating area; the kitchen would be slightly larger and there would be room for an additional loo. Having seen our way forward, we could go ahead with applying for planning permission, consulting the neighbours and, most important, fund-raising.

For the latter we set up yet another committee. They designed our 'bursting at the seams' leaflet and off it went to all the grant-making trusts they could think of and to every other Quaker meeting in the country. Having sent these appeals far and wide, back at home we organised our own small-scale efforts, right down to collecting jars of five pence pieces.

A further committee was appointed to co-ordinate our colour scheme. It was their task to choose such things as carpet tiles and curtains.

Meanwhile we continued our Meetings for Worship on Sundays. Our user groups were able to go on with their activities, cheerfully putting up with the sound of power drills, saws and hammers during working hours.

After weeks of viewing the new extension, first through a peephole in a temporary partition and then actually being allowed to walk round the inside, you can imagine our joy when we held our first Meeting for Worship there.

One more committee had to be appointed, its purpose being to make arrangements for the opening events. The first will be an Open Day on Saturday 12th October from 11 a.m. to 4 p.m., when everyone is welcome.

And now it is time to reveal the third reason for selecting our architect. On our very first meeting with him, he asked us what kind of space we wanted to create, and we replied, 'peaceful and welcoming'. We hope that this is what our many friends will experience when they come to see it for themselves.

Community Spirit (August 2007)

In tackling such a wide ranging and deep subject, I'll risk giving a couple of definitions. By community, I mean any group of people living, working or worshipping together. In his book *Utopian Dreams* (published in 2007) Tobias Jones describes his search for a better life, during which he visits New Earswick and particularly Hartrigg Oaks. More generally, he writes: 'Our society is, by now, so atomised, privatised and individualised that most people under, say, thirty, have no idea of what a community, a real community, is truly like. I, along with most of my peers, had only heard of this quaint idea from the wistful descriptions of elders who had grown up in one.'

To this I would reply that our memories can be very selective. Throughout my childhood years we camped in the Lake District for six weeks every summer and yet I do not now remember a single rainy day! So perhaps the 'wistful descriptions' mentioned above are seen through rose-tinted spectacles. It would be wiser to concentrate upon the here and now: things ain't what they used to be, and communities change.

Graeme Tiffany, of the Community Philosophy Project, gave a good example of this in one of his talks. He recalled the times when, as a nine-year-old, he spent happy days with his grandfather and his contemporaries in a shed at the allotments. There was a strong sense of community generated by working together. Yet when Graeme visited the area years later, it was deserted and overgrown with weeds. He found that new allotments were flourishing elsewhere, worked by men **and** women, young **and** old.

How should 'spirit' be defined? Its derivation from the Latin *spirare* (to breathe) is useful in this context. For what characterises the 'real community' is its breath of life, its animation.

At the discussion on community spirit held by the Community Philosophy Project we considered how life is breathed into communities when there is something to celebrate. And there have been plenty of these occasions in New Earswick in recent years: centenaries of the village, of the Trust, and of the Folk Hall, not forgetting the millennium, have been celebrated in different ways.

How many of these events were organised from 'the top down', (i.e. by the Joseph Rowntree Housing Trust) is difficult to judge. The number of groups taking part in the concert *This is us* at the Folk Hall was impressive and the co-ordination worked very smoothly. It brought home to me the fact that New Earswick consists of a cluster of small communities, most of them working from the grass roots up. The millennium itself inspired a street party in Ivy Place, organised solely on a neighbourhood basis.

In *Utopian Dreams*, Tobias Jones deplores the fact that 'we no longer feel the natural rhythms of the earth.' He continues, 'We no longer have the seasonal highs and lows, the sowing and the harvesting.' We do still have them, but they've changed their nature. Harvest festivals and Hallow E'en have been hi-jacked by the mischief-makers, for example. Declining church attendance has resulted in Easter becoming a matter of hot cross buns and chocolate eggs; the true meaning of Christmas is in danger of being swallowed up by consumerism. Remembrance Day, on the other hand, remains a powerful factor in the growth of community spirit. The moving ceremony at New Earswick Primary School will surely have a lasting effect on many of its pupils.

Community spirit is manifested in other ways too. It prompted the action of residents petitioning First York to restore the route of the number 12 bus service through the village. The campaign to have a 'lollipop person' on duty at the Primary School is another example of the community in action. Nor is it all local; the plight of people elsewhere in the world brings out our community spirit as we saw in the spontaneous response to the tsunami disaster of 2005.

Every month the 'freebie' *Local Link* advertises events in **other** villages – art exhibitions, concerts, carnivals, plays, treasure hunts, scarecrow trails, strawberry teas, table top sales and so on. All these activities are run by communities for the benefit of those communities. Why is this so? Is it because in the absence of a benevolent landlord, they simply have to do it themselves? But isn't that what community spirit is all about?

CHAPTER NINE

Personal Reminiscences

Getting to Know Mr Minney   (March 2007)

Writing about the early buses in last month's *Bulletin* made me want to know more about Mr Minney who, as a Parish Councillor, did so much to improve the service for the residents of New Earswick.   He is richly remembered by many, and the following article relies heavily on letters to me from his son Ralph.

Ralph's father, Arthur, was born near Northampton in 1892, but by the time he was old enough to go to school the family had moved to Market Harborough. One of his school reports read 'Arthur is very good at arithmetic, but mental also'!   His mathematical ability was also remarked upon at his next school, and eventually he qualified as a mechanical engineer.

When the 1914 War broke out he refused, as a Quaker, to be employed in the production of metal for weapons of war, and so he applied for a job at Rowntree's in York. On arriving at York Station and walking under the city walls, he saw all the daffodils in bloom and said to himself, 'Here I will stay' – and he did. Apparently there was a great need in both world wars for the troops to have chocolate bars and these were supplied by Rowntree's.   In the Second World War, he was involved in the mechanical technology for producing and packing chocolate for the Burma Campaign. It stayed solid up to 120° Fahrenheit (about 50° C) – and had an awful taste!

In 1919 he married Mabel Whitwell and they later moved to Park Avenue, to one of the houses backing on to two great cornfields, where Hartrigg Oaks now stands. The house cost £500 with parquet floor and large garage. They named it Muskoka after the lake north of Toronto, one of the many places that Arthur visited in his travels for Rowntree's.

For two years he shuttled to and fro by boat and train, on loan for short periods to Hersey's chocolate factory. After World War Two he was sent to Toronto to install equipment in Rowntree's factory there. His pre-war work took him to France and Germany as well. He also planned and equipped creameries in Ireland, and in the Lake District and Northumberland.

It is hardly surprising, then, that he enjoyed long walks and became interested in flowers and photography. Besides that, he was a very good footballer, tennis player, ballroom dancer and a skilful woodworker – 'certainly a Renaissance man,' as his son says.

Ralph's description of the war years in New Earswick casts an interesting light on its effects on the civilian population. For instance, he understands that his father initiated work with Italian and German prisoners of war on farms, particularly at Storwood in the East Riding. For this he was given a petrol allowance. It led to lasting friendships and also the formation of a camp orchestra.

As a senior ARP warden, writes Ralph, his father 'had a telephone installed. He was away two or three nights each week. Many a night we were rushed to our street air raid shelter.' A bomb landed by chance in the middle of the fields at the back of the garden. 'A few seconds earlier, it would have been New Earswick; a few seconds later, Park Avenue. Thank goodness it had been raining a lot; soil was hurled round in the crater, and the explosion was contained.'

Not long before D-day, Ralph remembers there being lots of American soldiers around. They were well supplied with nylon stockings which they insisted on giving away; they were sure everyone had a sister or a friend with sisters. 'No matter what you said, you ended up with a handful of them.' Ralph took his home to his mother who sold them to buy knitting wool to make balaclavas for the Russians.

As an experienced bee-keeper, his father was appointed inspector for a sickness called 'foul brood'. He also had to see that the allocation of 1-cwt bags of sugar was used only for the production of honey. His own bee-keeping continued for long after the war, and he used to take his bees on to the moors each summer for heather honey. Indeed by the late 1980s he had accrued enough honey in his roof to keep him going for ten years!

It was a hot summer when he died, in 1989, and the jars of honey had expanded and were leaking. You can imagine what happened: 'Bees a-buzzing – it was like a station in hell!' remembers Ralph. But he remembers so much more besides, far more than I can write here; his father was a truly remarkable man.

Return to New Earswick (December 2002)

What is it like for someone who spent his early days in New Earswick to retire here after being away for over 50 years? In Harry Crann's case it wasn't a complete absence, for he returned on many occasions to visit his mother, Ina, until her death in 1974. But that still leaves a memory gap of nearly 30 years.

Harry was born at 61 Hawthorn Terrace, and in about 1936 the family (mother, father, older sister Margaret and Harry) moved to 48 Hawthorn Terrace. Besides being a bigger house, it had the great attraction for Harry and his father of being nearer the Cricket Field – what today we call the Old School Playing Field, but as the Joseph Rowntree School hadn't then been built, it was simply 'the Cricket Field'.

Harry's father, Thomas William Crann (known as Billy to the family and as Tommy to his friends), was a research chemist in the laboratories at Rowntree's. He used to cycle to work, as did every one else – hardly anyone owned or used a car in those days, Harry told me. That's one of the biggest differences he notices.

When Harry was a boy, the road north from York more or less petered out in Haxby.   Harry remembers that there were only a few houses in The Village, plus the church, the school, and one shop – and that was it.

By contrast, New Earswick was much better off for shops. Counting from the post office, there was Mr Kay's grocery, followed by Miss Fairweather's confectionery and lastly the Co-op.   Round the corner was the quadrant of 'new' shops: a pharmacist where the newsagent now is, the Co-op butchery, then Burrell's bakery and lastly a hairdresser.

Down at the Station Avenue end of Chestnut Grove were more shops: another hairdresser, a cobbler and a haberdashery.   Harry particularly remembers Mr Bradley's hairdressing establishment for its mirrors. These were fixed on the end walls opposite each other, and Harry used to be fascinated by the endless reflections of himself in these two mirrors – receding in a curve to the left because the walls weren't quite parallel! Chestnut Grove itself was lined with horse chestnut trees in those days and there was keen competition every autumn to get the best conkers.

Talking of conkers reminded Harry of other childhood pastimes, particularly roller-skating down the pavement in Lime Tree Avenue. The paving slabs were very evenly laid, and the joints between them were slightly spaced. Skating over these produced a very satisfying clatter with the increase in speed, going downhill from what is now White Rose Avenue to the main road. (Harry assured me this is the only 'hill' in New Earswick!)

The way down would have taken Harry and his friends past the children's playground on their right, with a slide and what they called the 'lemon squash'. Beyond the Methodist Chapel was the original Red Lodge. Before it was replaced, this was a three-storeyed double-fronted house with rooms to let for single women, like Miss Gurney who taught at the school.

Harry doesn't remember many heavy falls of snow, with snowmen or snowball fights. He does, however, recall some very hard frosts when the brickyard pond froze over and they went skating.

Christmases were fairly quiet and family-centred. His parents set up the Christmas tree (a real one, of course) in one of the alcoves on either side of the fireplace. It was planted in a galvanised bucket wrapped round with coloured paper to make it look festive. Harry still remembers the amazement with which he opened his 'best' present: a Pullman coach and a locomotive for his Hornby train set. It had been bought from another family whose children had outgrown it – quite the usual practice in those days, all part of being a community.

Since returning to New Earswick, the memories have been coming back. Harry singled out the gym classes which he attended from about the age of seven on Monday evenings. They were run at the school by Mr

Pulleyn, who lived in Park Avenue. Once a year they put on a display for parents, enabling the children to show off their skills on the wall bars, the ropes and the balance beam, to say nothing of leaping from the spring board and over the vaulting horse. He now remembers all this with great joy. No wonder he is glad to be back.

Wartime Wedding   (April 2002)

6th April is a very special day for Mrs Marjorie Jones of Red Lodge: in 1945, it was the occasion of her marriage to Glyn Jones.   It had been a wonderful spring and Marjorie still remembers the amazement on the faces of Glyn's parents when they first saw the masses of daffodils on the bank below the city walls. The wedding day itself was beautiful with clear blue skies. The cherry trees, which then grew in a row in front of the Folk Hall, were in full bloom as Marjorie and her father walked from Beechwood, their home at 3 Station Avenue – just around the corner.

Marjorie had deliberately chosen ten o'clock on a Monday morning for her wedding because she wanted it to be a quiet one. She thought most people would be at home doing their washing. Not a bit of it; as she went into the Little Hall (now the Coffee Lounge), she saw the place was crowded with friends, relatives and well-wishers.

Looking at her marriage certificate, which measures about 20 inches by 24, Marjorie and I counted 64 signatures. As is customary at Quaker weddings, every one present signed the certificate and many of the names will be familiar to *Bulletin* readers. Besides members of the bride's family (Marjorie's maiden name was Wragge) and those of the groom, there are the names of Robert W. Rose, Alice (his wife) and Brian L. Rose.   Ken

Blanchard was there with his father William, so was Joan Burrell (now Joan Judge) and Harry Crann's mother, Ina.   Other well-known New Earswick figures included Mrs Sorensen of White Rose Dairy and the talented Nene Schwabe who used to teach dancing.

As it was war-time and clothing was still on coupons, the bride couldn't have everything new for her wedding outfit.   (At least she knew her shoes would be comfortable!) She did have a new dress and jacket of silky blue material, which she tells me she wore many times afterwards. Instead of carrying a bouquet, she pinned a spray of lilies of the valley to her jacket. A new hat was out of the question, and so she made do with an arrangement of white veiling on her brown hair.   Her white gloves had been specially crocheted for her by her mother-in-law to be.

After the simple exchange of vows, and the signing of the certificate, the sliding doors leading to the serving area were opened and everyone tucked in to the light refreshments which had been prepared by Mrs Lister. Even though most of the ingredients for the wedding cake were still rationed, Mr Kruger from the village had managed to make a big round cake, single-tiered and beautifully iced.

The only thing that didn't work out as planned was that the photographer never turned up.   Apparently he couldn't believe that a wedding would actually take place in a village hall, instead of a church or a chapel, and so he ignored the booking. (Before they had their own meeting house, New Earswick Quakers always held meeting for worship in at the Folk Hall so it was quite in order for them to have weddings there.)   Fortunately, Rendell Ridges was among those present and as he had brought his camera with him, he took an informal photograph of the newly-weds.

Marjorie and Glyn had met each other while they were both working at hostels which were run by the Friends' Relief Service. As conscientious objectors, that had been their war work. They were only allowed a few days' leave for their honeymoon, which was to be in Edinburgh. Off they went to the station to catch the train from London. Being war-time, it was absolutely packed and many people were sitting on their cases in the corridor. The young couple did manage to find seats in the same compartment, but not together. As they looked round at the other passengers, they thought one of them had a familiar face and then they realised it was Emlyn Williams, the famous actor and playwright! He and the rest of the cast appeared very tired (even a bit scruffy, according to Marjorie) and they slept for most of the journey.

Although Marjorie's brother, Philip, and her sister, Winifred, had attended the wedding, her other brother, Dennis, had not been able to come. He was serving as an officer in the Navy and couldn't get leave. So Marjorie and Glyn were delighted when Dennis' ship sailed into Leith during their stay in Edinburgh, and they were able to see him after all.

In spite of food rationing, clothing coupons, and the difficulties of arranging leave, Marjorie and Glyn had had a wonderful wedding.

Ian Cottom Remembers   (February 2002)

"Thanks for the Memory" as the old tune goes – perhaps it's just me, or is it merely an ageing syndrome one goes through as time slides by?

My thoughts turn to earlier days in New Earswick and a surge in nostalgia for the 'nice' old times with their attendant disciplined values which creep into our musings.

Happy days!   I hardly remember a time when we 'children of the village,' with our limited leisure facilities in the era before the Lime Tree Avenue playground, where the flats now stand, failed to enjoy ourselves. Bored! We never used that word. We used to make our own amusements and did we have fun!

I remember the wonderfully elaborate dug-out camps on the site of the old tip; complete with film shows (one cigarette card for admission!) also on hand was a clay fireplace to cook our own baked potatoes. I think of the trolleys made out of a plank and a few old boxes and pram wheels; home-made canvas canoes precariously paddled down the river; games of marbles on every street corner; whips and tops, boolers, scary dark evening dashes down the nackey path (exclusive to New Earswick), 'Kilvo's' ice cream tricycle, piles of leaves in autumn to make dens – one could go on for ever about those seemingly always sunny days – joyful days, in this once family-oriented village.

The primary school, or elementary school as it was known, is remembered with some affection by many of us 'oldies'.   Mrs Townshend's reception class; the clay dustbin, the inkpot desks – two seats to one desk – 'Gaffer' Barnes's chases around the cloakroom with a slipper for the unfortunate slowcoach!   Many other classroom memories will come to readers' minds.

Dig for Victory 'lessons' in the school gardens were most popular with the top two classes and it was 'hands-up any volunteer,' which shortened our education somewhat at the age of twelve!

Quite a few of my former classmates are still around in the New Earswick area and there is a positive warmth in our collective memories when we meet at the shops or wherever.

Some families moved further afield after World War Two, and one which I have kept in touch with since childhood days are the Pollards. Contemporary with me is Gerry and readers who remember them may be surprised to know that it is fifty years ago this month since the family (with the exception of Ken) – all seven of them, plus Kitty, Gerry's wife, packed their bags and emigrated to Australia. The headlines in *The Yorkshire Herald* at the time said "12,000 Miles To Give Family A Chance". A new life awaited them in faraway Longreach, Queensland, quite a change from the temperate clime of New Earswick.

Mr and Mrs Pollard died some years ago, also Gerry's brothers Val and more recently, Eric. Gerry and family live in Brisbane. His sisters Janet and Judy both live in that vicinity of Queensland. Another brother, Chris, lives in Wollongong, New South Wales. If anyone would like to get in touch I would be happy to supply addresses.

Finally, who said, "Nostalgia is a thing of the past?" Enjoy it, I do!

Mrs Audrey Cooper's Memories (April 2002)

Thank you, Ian Cottom, for that evocation of childhood in New Earswick. I also remember it with happy memories.

The lovely walks by the River Foss to Huntington. The stream on the left of the river with frogspawn and newts and fields of buttercups and milkmaids in the boggy patches.   In winter it would freeze on these fields where it was boggy, and those of us who were lucky would ice-skate here, but most of us just made slides and had sledges (mine was the airing-cupboard shelf).   I remember the long slides we made down Chestnut Grove in frosty weather.   There were long queues to have a go.

I remember the summer days in Magson's Field, which is where the Huntington [School] Sports Field is now.   It was a lovely hay meadow full of wild flowers and hedgerows of wild roses and crab-apples.   Every day seemed lovely weather in the summer, and we would paddle in the River Foss, which had a lovely sandy bottom and clear water, and down by the lock-house were many dragon-flies.

Our Milkman was Mr Broadley from Huntington with his horse and cart.   Sometimes we would ask him for a ride and help him deliver the milk.   It was ladled into customers' jugs and he always used to say, 'Give them a little extra.'

He was a large man and when he put one foot on the step of the cart, down it went and up went the front. 'Gee up!' and off we went back to his farm and he would give us free milk and plums off his trees.   Then we would walk home and cross the stepping-stones at Mill Hill and home along the river.

I have fond memories of the playground in Lime Tree Avenue.   I spent many happy hours there.   We would take polish and dusters to shine the chute (slide).   Mr Gresham would come and close the park at 8.00 p.m. in summer, and when he'd gone we would climb over the gate for an extra hour. That's about the worst thing we ever did in those days.

In winter months there was a monthly film show in the Folk Hall's small hall and monthly dramas in the large hall. Later there were the Gilbert and Sullivan Operas. Nearly all the village turned out to see these, and many of us took part.

I also well remember going to Sunday School at the Chapel. Once a year was the outing to the coast for the day. We all went to the village station, where we caught the train to Bridlington and after a good day out, came home tired and sun-burnt.

Then every year we had a village carnival. All the children were in fancy dress and some of the adults too. Mr Griffiths the local coalman always dressed up, and we used his coal-cart, all decorated up, to parade the Carnival Queen. Then at Christmas there was always a big party for the children in the Folk Hall.

In 1939 when the war broke out, we all had evacuees from Hull and Middlesbrough. A lot of them went home after a while, and we then had airmen and WAAFs billeted on to us. We had four airmen at our house, and they remained friends for life. They used to visit us for years after the war.

Happy memories!

Vonnie McCartney's Memories (June 2002)

Reading the letter in April's Bulletin from Mrs Audrey Cooper, I thought I might add my two pennyworth of memories of a happy childhood in New Earswick – but first of all, with my apologies to Audrey, the Chapel Sunday School outing went to Scarborough, not Bridlington (but I am of course open to correction). Also in connection with Sunday School were the pantomimes each year, run by the late Mrs Elsie Chown with great dedication and, I am sure, a lot of blood, sweat and tears. I also seem to remember our well-known ex-Primary School teacher, Miss Margaret Dufton, and the then Miss Joyce Barclay, in leading parts.

Then there were the Annual Anniversaries when, all dressed up in our Sunday best dresses (mine and my elder sister, Doreen's, were made each year by our Grandma Day) our hair curled by tongs, and sporting a satin ribbon, we sat up on the stage nervously hoping we would not forget the words to our recitations and solos. Trying not to giggle as we eagerly looked for our parents in the audience. Another treat was the prize-giving awarded for attendance, this was ascertained by the number of stars in our star card, which determined the quality of the book each child received. O.K., so today's children will without a doubt think, 'How boring', but not so the children of the 1930's and I for one would not change places as our lives seemed very full and happy.

How many of us, I wonder, remember Mr Page the Librarian who, I was sure, must have been at least a hundred years old in my childish thoughts, but he also seemed to have an unlimited number of sweets in his pocket, admittedly mostly Rowntree fruit gums with fluff stuck to them, but we didn't care!

At the risk of becoming boring, my friend Mrs Joyce Daniel and I were trying to think how many ladies in their early to mid-seventies whose parents and grandparents all lived in the village, are still living here. These are all we could name: Mrs Sylvia Moss and Mrs Audrey Cooper (cousins) whose grandparents were Mr & Mrs Goddard; Mrs Sheila Bunce, granddaughter of Mr &

Mrs Woodcock; Mrs Joyce Daniel, granddaughter of Mr & Mrs Nicholson; plus myself, the granddaughter of Mr & Mrs Day. All these grandparents must obviously have been among the first tenants in the village. Sorry to anyone I have missed out, but no doubt you will put me right. I suppose our roots must go very deep or perhaps we are just old stick-in-the-muds. Of course many of our age married and moved away in the years just after the war, and some left to live abroad as £10 emigrants.

P.S. Going back maybe twenty years, at the request of the late Mrs Joan Ashmore the then Librarian, I wrote a quite comprehensive account of childhood in New Earswick for use in the Library. I wonder if anyone knows what happened to it?

[We are happy to be able to tell Mrs McCartney that with the efficient help of the Joseph Rowntree Foundation Library, we have discovered a copy of that account, which is reproduced below – *Editors*]

Memories of Childhood in New Earswick in the 1930s

Having lived in New Earswick for all bar the first eighteen months of my life, I have seen many changes take place. I must agree when I hear people say how lucky our children are to be growing up in this lovely village with all its modern amenities, but I wonder, are they really any happier with their rather sophisticated upbringing, than I, and many more like me were forty or even more years ago.

My home, until the day I married, was at 19 Ivy Place and will always hold many happy memories for me. The long back garden with its two apple trees, plum tree and numerous soft fruit bushes went straight down to the River Foss in which we spent many happy hours paddling and fishing in the clean water. I certainly do not remember hearing anything about pollution, there was even a stretch a little further up that people actually swam in. What fun we had playing tracking among all the back lanes and the so-called "nackey path" which now forms part of the new road running from the shops between the back gardens of the beginning of Chestnut Grove and Hawthorn Terrace. Then there was the swing park in Lime Tree Avenue, now occupied by a block of flats. How daring of us to hide on the top of the chute when we saw "old Mr Gresham" coming to lock the gate as dusk fell. I do not think we ever got the better of him as he knew us all too well, as did Mr Armstrong, the village policeman, who would not be averse to giving us a clip round the ear if we ever did anything really bad, or even worse, he might go and tell our parents, and believe me, he knew just where each and everyone of us lived.

I wonder how many people can recall the names of the local tradesmen with their horses and carts, all so very much a part of our village life. There was Mr Griffiths with his coalcart, Mr Gates the butcher, his cart was complete with chopping block, where he cut up the meat in the winter months, by the light of beautifully polished lamps attached to the back of the cart. What a treat to have a ride in Mr Broadley the milkman's horse and trap. I can still picture it today, with its churns and measuring jugs.

Saturday night was bath night. The old-fashioned gas copper in the kitchen was lit and filled up with water, and while it was heating, the bath top which was used as a table, was cleared, and when lifted up revealed what must rate as the biggest porcelain bath I have ever seen. I believe there were only two like that in the village. At this time I was the youngest of three children, so I was the first to be bathed, then while I was dried in front of a lovely coal fire, into the bath went my elder sister and another couple of pans full of hot water, followed by the same procedure for my big brother. Not very hygienic some may think, but as there was no running hot water in those days, this was the accepted thing on bath nights, and we certainly suffered no ill effects.

Sundays saw us all dressed up in our best clothes with our hair curled up with the curling tongs ready for Sunday School in the afternoon. We were never allowed to go out to play on Sundays. Perhaps when the weather was fine our parents would be waiting for us when we came out of Sunday School and we would go for a walk through the pea and bean fields (opposite the Joseph Rowntree School) and over the monkey stiles across the railway lines and then on to Wigginton Road. Not for us the luxury of a Sunday car ride to the coast.

The highlight of the year came in June, when we went on the Sunday School trip to Scarborough. Up bright and early and down to Earswick station, where our special train was waiting. No worries about the weather as I am sure that the sun always shone for us, which is just as well, as all we wanted was the sea and sand, and perhaps if we were lucky a ride on the swing-boats, and of course piles of sandy egg sandwiches. Home tired and happy, and maybe as a special treat we would stop on the sleeper path for a pennorth of chips from Harry Bradley's, and then there was Mr Willey to call "goodnight" to as we passed him still at work in his cobbler's shop, where the Estate Office now stands.

Thinking back, I must also mention the Pantomimes I took part in every winter. These were produced by the late Mrs Elsie Chown. What patience she must have had with us budding young actors and actresses. I think she must have loved us almost as much as we loved her. I can still recall the smell of the grease paint and feel the thrill and excitement of the footlights on "The Night".

Finally let us take a stroll along the main road and see what changes have taken place in the intervening years. The only school then was the present Junior school which to my mind has changed very little over the years. Whenever I have gone back with my own children, the years have slipped away and I could almost see Mr Thomas Barnes stood at the door of the Headmaster's Office watching us file along the corridor. A little further along the Post Office as it is today, but then it was run by Mr & Mrs Walt Pawson. Next door, Mr Kay the village grocer and then Miss Fairweather in her sweet shop and last of all, the Co-operative Stores, but then it had two long counters with a chair or two for the customers, and of course, sawdust on the floor. In the house where Mrs Joan Armstrong now lives, lived Doctor Riddolls and his family. I should imagine the majority of the residents in those days were the patients of Doctor Riddolls. The next house was the home of Doctor Gaynor, and it was in his garden that the snowdrops and aconites were to me the first signs of Spring. Looking back I always thought Doctor Gaynor must be about a hundred years old, he wasn't of course, but that is how he appeared to me as a child. He always had time to show us round his garden and tell us the names of all the flowers and plants. Where the "Garth" now stands was the farm of Mr & Mrs Sorenson and its adjoining fields, on which is now built White Rose Avenue.

As a closing memory, as a very small child I can just remember being taken for a walk as far as Rowntrees, and there being taken for a ride on the top of a tram car, but it is all very vague. No doubt someone a little older than me, could tell us a little more about them.

Happy Shopper   (April 2004)

Our readers will be aware that on 8 March 2004 Geoff Howard retired after 34 years at the Happy Shopper. Pictured here with the new proprietors, Ashley Hetherington and Kirsty Plant, Geoff writes as follows:

I feel that I must put pen to paper to thank everyone who has made my job the best job you could have. Where else can you laugh and make money for twelve hours a day?

In 1937 I was born in New Earswick and lived at 9, Lime Tree (Happy Days!) playing Cowboys and Indians, whip & top, hop scotch, pinching a few apples and plums until the local 'bobby' caught you, clipped your ear and took you home – then your dad clipped you again! German planes dropping bombs in the fields behind our house (they just missed the chippie) on Sleeper Path. Being in Air Raid shelters all over the village or hiding under the kitchen table, every villager helping each other.

Off to New Earswick Primary school – what fun! I loved my teacher Margaret Dufton. Still do! Then there was Ma Jenkins. Did I respect her! She also taught you to respect other people. Were we scared of her! Told me I had no prospect at all. I wish she was alive today – I think I proved her wrong. I remember the headmaster whacked my backside and I wet myself. My mam went to see him. Bet she told him.

Then I went to Joseph Rowntree. I got a good report for football when I left. Mr Duckworth was the headmaster then. Mr Slack, Mr Lightowler, Ossie Smith, Mr Stewart, Mr Glasby, Flash Gordon, Mr Appleby and Mr Whithorn; these, to name a few, were my tops for the best with that cane! They certainly taught me respect if nothing else.

In 1952 I left school and got a job at New Earswick Co-op. It was all I ever wanted to do. I got myself a new bike to deliver orders on (Granville, eat your heart out). A few years on and round the village with that electric van, selling bread and cakes made in the Co-op. Lovely they were.

In 1960 I married my lovely wife, Maureen. Over the years I have had five great kids. How I found the time I just don't know. My neighbour at the time, in Lime Tree, Harry Pawson, had a mobile van selling around the Selby area. 'Take this round off me, Geoff,' he said. So I did. Ten years of long hours! Thanks, Harry.

Then, by chance, my wife saw an ad in the Estate Agents, 'Empty Shop in New Earswick'. I walked round all the banks in York trying to borrow £250, but to no avail. My last bank, the Midland on Nessgate Corner, said 'yes,' and away I went... Thirty-four years later I am now retiring. I have had a brilliant time. There have been some lovely customers and top staff. But now I have free time for me and my wife, and get to go away with the caravan.

I will miss you all as I go whistling into the sunset...

Jon Barker-Wyatt   (September 2000)

It was with great sadness that New Earswick residents learned that Jon Barker-Wyatt had died on Sunday 6th August 2000.

Jonathon had worked for the Trust for over 10 years, and had made many friends amongst the residents of New Earswick and throughout the Trust's other areas. He worked tirelessly, with quiet determination and dedication, to promote resident involvement and participation. Many of us will remember him for his quiet presence, his eye for detail and his willingness to listen to others' points of view.

Family, friends and colleagues attended a Thanksgiving Service at Copmanthorpe Methodist Church on Friday 11th August.

A Memorial Service for Jon, open to all residents, friends and colleagues, will be held at The Folk Hall on Friday 15th September, 2.00 - 3.00 p.m.

Jon's Nature Walk – from the JRHT (August 2001)

The working group which is establishing a nature walk as a memorial to Jon Barker-Wyatt, applied for a donation to cover the costs of installing 2 more benches along this new walk. The Joseph Rowntree Foundation has already donated £10,000 and the laying of the paths is being undertaken by the British Trust for Conservation Volunteers. £700 was agreed to be our contribution to this worthy venture.

(September 2001)

Claire Barker-Wyatt and Cedric Dennis officially opened the Jon Barker-Wyatt Memorial Nature Walk on Monday 6 August 2001, the first anniversary of Jon's death. Over 70 family, friends, residents and colleagues gathered at the Folk Hall, on a rainy afternoon to look at displays of the walk under construction and a pictorial history of areas of the walk, over a cup of tea and a piece of cake.

Nigel Naish (Trustee) and Cedric Dennis (Director of Care Services) welcomed everyone, thanked all those people who had been involved, especially Rosie Wright from New Earswick Primary School, whose squirrel logo was selected to mark the way along the route. After the ribbon cutting people had a chance to walk along the route.

All those who participated agreed that the walk was a fitting memorial to Jon.

Wyn Ogley – by the Editorial Sub-group (December 2001)

It is with much regret that we report the death of Wyn Ogley on 3 November 2001. As many people in the village will be aware, Wyn was a much respected and busy member of the community right up to the time of her death.

Wyn lived all her life in New Earswick. She was born in 1915, the daughter of Mr Griffiths, the village coal merchant, who also kept pigs and hens on a smallholding very close to St Andrews Church.

In her early life she attended the New Earswick village school, leaving at the age of fourteen. During this period she learned to play the piano and this provided her with much pleasure throughout the rest of her life.

Wyn was married to Bill and had two children, Neil and Jean. Sadly Wyn was widowed in 1964 at the age of 49, leaving her with the care of the two children, aged 12 and 16.

As her children required her attention less Wyn joined in Village activities in a big way. Some of her interests were: Treasurer of the Ebor Wine Circle, producer of the Ebor Tipplers, Secretary to the Yorkshire Wine Federation, Treasurer to Tadcaster Carnival Committee, Meals on Wheels, Samaritans, Village Council and Huntington Whist Drive. This village benefited directly as Wyn was one of the founder members of the bowls club at New Earswick Folk Hall. She also held the positions of Chairman and Treasurer of the Pensioners' Association and was a member of the New Earswick Pensioners' Whist Drive.

In her later years Wyn thoroughly enjoyed organising an annual pensioners' holiday and many day outings. She also enjoyed being a member of the York branch of Cruse, belonging to the Theatre Club and being Chairman and Treasurer of the New Earswick Disabled Club. In addition to all of this, during her retirement Wyn spent more than ten years working voluntarily in a Help the Aged shop.

Her family are grateful for the support and affection of the community in which she was so closely involved for so many years.

Barbara Wrigglesworth – by the Editorial Sub-group (August 2003)

Barbara Wrigglesworth died at the age of 63 in York District Hospital on Wednesday 9th July, peacefully after a long illness. She had spent most of her married life in New Earswick and was well known and liked in the village. Residents in Hawthorn Terrace, Chestnut Grove and Ivy Place will remember with affection her kindness as a good neighbour, her concern for others in her work for Neighbourhood Watch, and the part she played in community events such as the Millennium celebrations.

Our deep sympathy goes out to her husband John and to all her family. They wish to express their thanks for all the cards and expressions of condolence they have received, and for the generosity of those who contributed to the collection for Cystic Fibrosis which was taken up in Barbara's memory.

Peter Spavin – by the Editorial Sub-group (May 2006)

We record with great sadness the sudden death of Peter Spavin on 11 April 2006. Peter was a talented organist whose playing enriched the worship of congregations at the New Earswick Methodist Church and at St Lawrence Church in York, and whose contributions to the New Earswick Musical Society were greatly valued.

He was also an energetic and punctilious Secretary of the New Earswick Residents' Forum from 2000 to 2004, and used his considerable skills in the field of information technology to the great benefit of many in New Earswick and beyond. He will be much missed, and we offer our sincere condolences to his Mother.

Farewell to Richard Best – by the Editorial Sub-group (December 2006)

At the end of December, Lord Richard Best will be retiring as Director of the Joseph Rowntree Foundation, a post he has held since 1988.

The Foundation is one of the largest social policy research and development charities in the UK, spending about £7 million a year on seeking ways to understand and overcome the causes of social difficulties, working in partnership with a large variety of academic and other institutions.

The Joseph Rowntree Housing Trust, established in 1968, is part of the Joseph Rowntree Foundation. It owns the freehold of nearly all the properties in New Earswick, and also carries out housing and care schemes elsewhere in York and Yorkshire. These are of a developmental nature, demonstrating new forms of tenure, meeting special needs and exploring new features of design, with the twofold objectives of social and environmental sustainability.

Most familiar to New Earswick residents is the continuing care retirement community of Hartrigg Oaks, now eight years old; but other new communities are continually being developed, and among these is Derwenthorpe, to be built on land to the east of York in partnership with the City of York Council. It will include rented and low-cost home ownership homes scattered among fully owner-occupied housing, and has been planned on sustainable, energy-friendly principles, with pedestrian-friendly streets, reduced traffic flow, secure homes and safe open spaces. It will have enhanced local transport systems including a car club, cycle ways and pedestrian links.

Further afield, in Hartlepool, is the planned development of Hartfields, an extra care retirement village consisting of 242 units of accommodation, where people aged 60 plus will be able to live independent lives in a socially supportive environment. Flexible financial options mean that housing will be available to purchase, part-own (shared ownership) or rent. The accommodation will be built to the 'Lifetime Homes' standard, helping people at any stage of the life-cycle to maintain independence; and there will be range of communal facilities including a restaurant, a health activity centre, a library and allotments.

The direction of such projects, and the development of the research and philosophical basis which underpins them, demands the simultaneous management both of broad strategic issues and of specific local details. In his long association with the Trust's original community of New Earswick, Lord Best has found useful experience of the way that its policies work out in practice, and this is a continuing process. A current example is the development of the Elm Tree Garage site (to be called Elm Tree Mews) which has offered the chance to experiment not only in the latest environmental techniques but also in design. Thus the building will benefit both from solar panels on the roof, and from heating piped up from 100m below the site; and while its design is modern, not a mere replica of what has gone before, its appearance is still in harmony with the existing aesthetic.

Other perennial New Earswick concerns continue to occupy his thoughts. Its pleasant open spaces are one of its most attractive features, but they are also vulnerable to periodic episodes of unacceptable behaviour, often on the part of people who are not New Earswick residents. Strategies for coping with this problem are permanently under review – the evaluation by Leeds University of the recent Dispersal Order is a case in point.

There is anxiety too about the plight of elderly people on fixed incomes, not in receipt of benefit, who face a rising burden of expenditure on rent.   The Foundation has promoted the use of leasehold schemes by which the elderly occupiers own 70% of the equity in their homes, while the landlord owns the other 30% and is able to buy back a proportion of the occupier's share if they need to unlock some of their capital in an emergency.   In New Earswick it operates a policy of offering for sale every alternate vacant property, to promote an equitable social mix of tenancy and owner-occupation in the community. The safeguards built in to this policy include the pledge to use the proceeds from sale to create other properties available for rent, a service charge payable by the purchaser to contribute to the upkeep of local amenities, and the Trust's first right to buy back the property if it is again offered for sale.

At the heart of these policies is the recognition that a secure affordable home, in a neighbourhood which improves rather than limits life chances, is fundamental to personal wellbeing.   The Foundation's ethos, stemming from the Quaker philosophy of its founder, is to see the best in people and trust them to make good use of the facilities it provides.

While at its head, Lord Best has been a good friend to New Earswick. Whether cutting the first slice at the Centenary Hog Roast, or chairing the discussion of the

Prime Minister's lecture at the Folk Hall, he has always placed high value on a good relationship with village residents. We shall miss him, and we wish him well as a champion in the House of Lords and in his new post as Chair of the Hanover Housing Association.

Richard Best cuts the first slice at the Joseph Rowntree Foundation's Centenary Hog Roast, September 2004.

CHAPTER TEN

Prospects for the
New Millennium

Julia Unwin Calls for a New Debate – by the
Editorial Sub-group (April 2007)

On Monday 19 March Julia Unwin, the new Director of
the Joseph Rowntree Foundation, addressed Hartrigg
Oaks residents. Her theme was Social Evils of the 21st
Century – what would concern Joseph Rowntree today?

Julia began by paying tribute to the careful thought and
patient evidence-gathering with which Joseph Rowntree
had addressed the social issues of his day, a tradition
which had been carried on by his Foundation ever since.

When in 1904 he set up his three Trusts to search out the
'underlying causes of weakness or social evil in the
community', he recognised that future perceptions of
these issues would change in the course of time. Now,
just over a century later, in the village that he created, it
was appropriate to start a new debate abut the nature of
social evil in the 21st century.

In this debate there would be more questions than
answers. We should not assume that we know what
people think, or the solutions to current problems. We
should go to schools, housing estates, prisons and places
of worship, the places where people meet, and the places
where they would never normally have the conversation,
and ask what is a social evil in our new century? What
are the things that would concern Joseph Rowntree if he
were around today?

Julia proposed to begin by raising some thought-provoking issues, beginning with a warning not to fall into the trap of looking back with nostalgic dissatisfaction to a time when things were better than they are now. For in many ways things have greatly improved since Joseph Rowntree's day. There has been enormous progress in issues such as religious tolerance, women's rights, health-care, education, housing and the avoidance of global conflict. The development of information technology enables us to access, marshal and analyse data in ways undreamt of in 1904.

Moreover, the new debate should not be held in the partisan arenas of religion, politics or administration. Rather, it should seize the imagination of all who take part in it, and allow us to take stock at the start of a new era, and to start to answer the question – how should we, Joseph Rowntree's heirs and successors, respond?

At the beginning of the twentieth century, people hoped for improvements in science, trade, democracy and government; and they were willing to listen to contrary points of view. The chief social evils that concerned Joseph Rowntree were ignorance, ill-health and idleness. It was for these reasons that his Trusts tried particularly to bring about improvements in education, housing and employment.

But what are the big issues of today? What, for example, are the evils that spring from our much greater affluence? Our excessive consumption has brought about a steep rise in environmental degradation, and its impact on the climate threatens not just how we live, but the very survival of future generations. It has also contributed to the growth in a number of different forms of addiction, and an ever more widespread dependency on alcohol and drugs of all kinds.

Is it too fanciful to attribute to affluence changes in the ways in which we view the next generation? Inter-generational tension is an issue affecting all western societies. In this country the paralysis that seems to afflict any discussion about meeting the costs of long-term care is a major manifestation of the tension between generations. In an affluent society the gulf between the rich and the poor threatens us all, making it harder for generations to work together.

And what of avarice? The slave trade, one of the greatest evils ever, was abolished in law two hundred years ago. But the trafficking in human misery has not ceased, and is driven by avarice. Is it avarice that allows us to treat others with contempt, indifference or hostility? How did it happen that the phrase 'asylum seeker' – so clearly a statement of fundamental human need – became a term of abuse?

Then consider apathy and anger. Within 24 years of Joseph Rowntree's original memorandum, we achieved universal suffrage in this country. Yet nowadays more people vote for Celebrity Big Brother than in local elections. The apathy which erodes engagement in the democratic process is a significant social evil. Across the country good and worthy attempts to engage people with the task of running their own services are met with apathy, and it is apathy that prevents the reporting of domestic violence and child abuse. The danger of such apathy was recognised by Edmund Burke in the 18th century, when he said, 'It is necessary only for the good man to do nothing for evil to triumph.'

Social evil is an uncomfortable term. Many of us would rather retreat to generalisations about social problems, and devise administrative responses. But the founder of the Joseph Rowntree Foundation and the sister Trusts saw the issues he was addressing as 'evils' – and brought to bear his own analytic powers, his life experience and his willingness to hear the voice of the dispossessed. Surely we, the inheritors of his concerns, can do no less than raise the question: 'What does social evil look like in this century?' and then use all our powers, our analytical ability, and our ability to persuade, to create responses to it.

The Joseph Rowntree Foundation is keen to hear your views on this topic. Please tell them what you think are the most important social evils affecting the United Kingdom today, and why you think they are important.

In January 2000 the New Earswick Community Association produced a special Millennium Bulletin, which included the following, penned by an anonymous resident:

Stargazing: What does the next 1000 years hold?

So, what can we expect at the end of the next Millennium? I suppose the one certainty is that none of us will be here to celebrate it! – but will Man have found the Elixir of Life? I doubt it, but I do believe that medical science will have progressed sufficiently to have eradicated most of the present day killers – cancer, AIDS, heart problems and so forth – although this may well be at the expense of a policy that allows only healthy foetuses to survive in the first place and euthanasia to be commonplace. I do, however, think that genetics will have made great strides so I would expect people may well be living to 150 to 200 years old.

If this is so, where will the increased population live? Well, of course the Moon will certainly be settled, together probably with Mars (and its two small moons Phobos and Deimos) – the Moon quite early in the Millennium, Mars much later.

And the earth itself will soon have to be governed by a Global Government which will see the sense of apportioning the land masses much more equally between the populations than is currently the case (always assuming that Global warming has left enough land to be shared out!). Normal problems of climate in relation to location will be of relatively minor importance as touch-sensitive, voice-controlled, thought-controlled computers with built-in intelligence keep temperature, humidity and other such piffling worries in order in buildings designed for the area in which they are to be erected and using appropriate materials. Our friendly benevolent Global Government would also have resolved the problem of equal distribution of wealth so worries over control of land or money would be a thing of the past.

Electronic communication will be taken for granted, but at the speed of light rather than bps. Rather, I suggest that our descendants may be surfing the Galaxy and inviting their friendly next door aliens for the weekend, assuming you believe, as I do, that other intelligent forms for life exist! And how would they get there? Well, depending on where they lived, perhaps a Number 12 Space shuttle or the long- distance Inter-Galactic Time Travel machine.

Nearer home I think we can expect inter Continental people and goods carriers using underground or overhead tubes with almost continuous high speed units within them. Nodes would enable them to be directed to major centres from which local, standing room only people carriers and small volume goods carriers would operate.

Would we work? Well obviously most of the routine stuff, like designing and building things would be automated, there wouldn't be any accompanying paperwork in a purely electronic world and intelligent robots would do so many of the present jobs we regard as chores. Humans, being as they are, would not wish to relinquish all control of machines, but as most machines would be 'intelligent', jobs for humans are going to be scarce. So what would be available to lower boredom level? Well there would always be visits to the nearest Moon Disney World or a voyage across the Sea of Tranquillity since quite a number of the *rilles* and *maria* will almost certainly have filled with water to make the moon habitable. For the more adventurous, perhaps a Spaceship to Venus or one of the more exotic satellites?

The human race itself will be capable of being cloned so that only the best strains will be preserved and birth itself will be a much simpler affair, probably equally shared between male and female since it is extremely unlikely that the present concept of 'Family' will mean very much in the new Millennium. Numbers will be strictly controlled, of course, but largely by the cloning and selection programme itself.

I would also predict that, at birth, all humans will have an implant into their brain which, in addition to carrying all their personal registration details, would operate by means of pulses that could either receive messages from the brain or send pulses to the brain using an array of data and information sources for educational purposes –

so potentially the knowledge and wisdom of the ages would be available at a thought.

Food as such could be a thing of the past with the availability of high nutrient mini capsules, but again human nature may well operate against the total abandonment of the 'look and smell' of real meals – at least in the Folk Hall! – and for special occasions.

The other stone cold certainty as we approach the end of the next Millennium is that MacMicroIntel Plc would have solved the latest Millennium bug problem with its introduction of Windows 3000 ver. 2 million.4.

Enough! It almost makes me pleased that I won't be here to enjoy it. But then, this is just one (moderately) old man's possibly rather jaundiced view!

Getting Stuck In – a few afterthoughts
(August 2000)

The conference held on 17th June, which went under this challenging but rather inelegant title, was full of interest and provided me, as an incomer, with plenty to think about.

Basically, 'getting stuck in' was about how community development can make a difference in places like New Earswick.

Besides being given a splendid lunch, we were supplied with various documents, one of which was a 70-page report covering progress in the last two years. If only we'd had time to read it before the conference, I am sure the discussion would have been more informed.

Anyway, here are a few *after* thoughts.

It is now nearly a hundred years since Joseph Rowntree began his garden village and his plan was that it should consist of about 100 houses; but it has since grown to 1,100. Surely the success of any community must be affected by its size, so I want to know if the academics who came to monitor our community know of any research on the optimum size.

I should think the stability of the population also has an effect. On a recent visit to Keswick, my husband and I came across an open shelter of the type being planned for the young people of New Earswick. There was a notice to say it had been constructed by the young people of Keswick in 1930. Most impressed by this, we enquired further, only to be told that the reason it was now under repair was because of vandalism by today's teenagers. I doubt whether any of the vandals belonged to the families of those 1930 youngsters.

A high population turnover must affect the spirit of a community and the sense of belonging. The rent records could provide such information for New Earswick and might help our understanding of what is happening. Since coming here, my husband and I have noticed that those who were born and bred in New Earswick are rightly proud of the fact – but how many of them are there, and what influence can they have?

Of course there must be change. There have been two wars since Joseph Rowntree began to make his dream come true. That's enough to shake up any community. So was the sudden loss of jobs when successive governments started to run down our railway system.

Perhaps even more important factors are the advent of the motor car and then of television. They've given us independence, which is great, but they've also caused communities to fragment. We are more confined to our little boxes, whether they be metal boxes on wheels or boxes of bricks and mortar. And what about the boxes within boxes, where many children now have their own TV sets in their bedrooms? I'm not saying that these advances are bad, but they must have an effect and I wonder how big that effect is and what can be done to counter it.

It's not just the community that keeps changing, it's the challenge.

ACKNOWLEDGMENTS

I am grateful for permission to include contributions from Joan Addison, Julie Boyes, Geoff Bunce, Colin Cameron, Audrey Cooper, Ian Cottom, Carole Farrar, Jonathan Gibson, Peter Giles, John & Enid Harrington, Geoff Howard, Brian Jardine, Elizabeth Jefferson, Michael Longhurst, Helen Mackenzie, Vonnie McCartney, New Earswick All Blacks, New Earswick Swimming Club, Ian Nicholson, Richard Revell, Sally Shaw, Peter Spavin, and Audrey Steel.

BIBLIOGRAPHY

Allott, Stephen
John Wilhelm Rowntree 1868-1905
(1994, Sessions of York, The Ebor Press)

Cocoa Works Magazine
(1902 *et seq.*, Rowntrees Cocoa Works)

Countryside Agency, The
Out in the Country
(2002, Countryside Agency Publications,)

Ellis, Jonathan (Policy Manager, Help the Aged)
in *Welfare Reform on the Web (January 2004): Care of the Elderly - UK*
(www.bl.uk/welfarereform/issue54/carelduk.html)

Fife, Michael G. & Peter J. Walls
The River Foss – its History and Natural History
(1981, Sessions of York, The Ebor Press)

Hartrigg Oaks News
(1998 *et seq.*, Hartrigg Oaks Residents' Association)

Haxby Town Council
2020 Vision: a plan for the future of Haxby
(2004, Haxby Town Council)

Howard, Ebenezer
The Garden Cities of Tomorrow
(1902, Swan Sonnenschein & Co. Ltd)

Jones, Tobias
Utopian Dreams
(2007, Faber and Faber)

Murphy, Joe
New Earswick, A Pictorial History
(1992, Sessions of York, The Ebor Press)

Nuffield Foundation
Old People: report of a survey committee on the problems of ageing and the care of old people
(1947, Oxford University Press; reprinted 1980)

Reader's Digest Nature Lover's Library
Field Guide to the Birds of Britain
(1981, Reader's Digest Association Ltd)

Field Guide to the Trees and Shrubs of Britain
(1981, Reader's Digest Association Ltd)

Waddilove, Lewis
One man's vision: the story of the Joseph Rowntree Village Trust
(1954, George Allen and Unwin)

Wagner, Gillian
The Chocolate Conscience
(1987, Chatto and Windus)

INDEX

41
Shaw, Sally 76
Sherriff & Mennell 63
Silva, Peter 114
Skelton 86
Slack, Mr 183
Sleeper Path Project 10, 78,
   112, 118, 137
Smith, Pam 15-16, 146,
   147, 157
Snowdon, Councillor 94-5
Solice, Gerry 16
Sorensen, Carl & Wilfred
   60-62
Sorensen, Mrs 171
Spavin, Peter 133, 135,
   187
St Andrew's church 66, 185
Stape 78
Station Avenue 28, 118,
   120, 155, 168, 170
St Lawrence's church 187
St Leonard's Hospice 158
Steel, Mrs Audrey 34
Stewart, Mr 183
Storwood 166
Strensall 45, 65, 76, 86
Suffragette campaign 69
Summer Scheme 106, 113
Swedish Flats 15
Sycamore Avenue 48, 86
Sycamore Flats 24

Tang Hall Community
   Centre 14
Tanner's Moat 5
Tanner's Yard 67
Taylor, John 26

Tebbutt, John 61
Tiffany, Graeme 163
TimeChange 149-52
Tomlinson, Linda 16
Townshend, Mrs 173
Triangular Meadow 53-4

Unwin, Julia 192-5

Venue, The 145
Vere, Erica 7
Victoria, Queen 34-5
Village Council 66, 68, 81
Village Trust, The 4, 23, 25,
   66, 92, 155

Waind, Lt Arthur 93
Waind, Mrs Edith Marion 93
Walls, Peter 31, 45-7
Ward Committee 87-8, 94,
   109-10
Ward, John 86
Ward, P.C. Dave 136
Wesleyan chapel 155-6
West Croft 93
West Huntington Hall 50
West Yorkshire Road Car
   Company 64
Western Terrace 2, 13, 15,
   27, 127
Westfield Beck 89-90, 102
Westfield House 30
White Rose Avenue 18, 39,
   40, 121, 169, 181
White Rose Dairy 60-61
White Rose Estate 61
White Rose Farm 39
Whithorn, Mr 183